BRAVELY LEADING

DARLIA CLARK

BRAVELY LEADING

WHERE FEAR MEETS FLIGHT

"Wherever you are right now, know this: you already have everything inside you to rise, rebuild, and bravely lead."

To my daughters,

and every little girl dreaming beyond her front porch:
Remember, fear will always be there, but you
must find the courage to move through it.

Chase your dreams anyway!

Independently Published

Copyright @ 2026 Darlia Clark

All rights reserved.

For permissions, contact:

Darlia Clark

Atlanta, Georgia

www.bravelyleadingbook.com

ISBN (Paperback): 979-8-9942648-2-9

ISBN (Hardback): 979-8-9942648-1-2

ISBN (eBook): 979-8-9942648-0-5

ISBN (Audio): 979-8-9942648-3-6

Printed in the United States of America

About the Author

Darlia Clark has spent over three decades leading some of the world's most significant brand transformations, stepping into high-stakes moments and turning corporate chaos into clarity (and occasionally into a good story). From makeup counters to major boardrooms, she's built her career on grit, grace, and a knack for finding opportunity in the unexpected.

Her path wound through retail aisles, corporate towers, motherhood, heartbreak, and even breast cancer, life's ultimate crash courses in courage. Along the way, she discovered that authentic leadership isn't about titles or corner offices, but about lifting others as you climb and keeping your sense of humor when things go sideways.

These days, Darlia is a speaker, mentor, and author, championing human-centered leadership and encouraging women to stand tall—even in rooms that weren't built for them. She lives in Atlanta with her husband, two daughters, and two dogs, all of whom remind her daily that resilience, laughter, and a little bit of chaos are ingredients for a life well led.

She's not done yet, Darlia's next adventure may be in the board room, on stage, the big screen, or anywhere courage and a good story need to be told.

Contents

Introduction

Don't you dare let fear stop you from rising in your life, your work, and into the person you were born to be.

Hello, y'all. I'm Darlia Clark, and I'm so glad you're here.

For those who don't know me, let me give you a little peek into why I decided to write Bravely Leading, Where Fear Meets Flight.

I'm just a girl from the small southern town of Cleveland, Tennessee, right outside Chattanooga. My parents raised us with two things: an undying work ethic and the reminder to have a little fun along the way.

My dreams have always ebbed and flowed. One day, I wanted to be a movie star; the next, a rock star, and then I thought if I could just get a job at the department store makeup counter, life would be complete. To me, those ladies had it all. They looked glamorous and helped other women feel their best. Looking back, I can trace my "goal size" right alongside my confidence level at the time.

The big dreams came early and, at times, were chipped away to almost nothing because life threw me plenty of curveballs. I had a lazy eye, glasses, a slight speech impediment, and more than a few battles with weight. Confidence didn't come easy, as I was no stranger to events that knock you down and strip you of that. One teacher tried to put me in special education because she thought I'd never be able to read or write. I thought cutting with scissors was hard enough. (Spoiler alert: I learned to cut with scissors. I just try not to run with them.) Luckily, my mom, who was both a schoolteacher and a firecracker, fought for me every step of the way. Years later, she had a chance to brag about me to that same teacher, and trust me, she did not hold back.

School had its ups and downs, too, especially being compared to my older brother. He was a star student, and if he struggled in a subject, I wasn't even given the chance. French was one of them. He had a hard time, so they told me I couldn't take it, but I convinced them otherwise and ended up doing just fine. I think that was partly because the subject interested me, but mostly because I love to prove a point through a little competition. Toward the end of high school, I was more than ready to be done, but my parents insisted on college.

One night while having dinner at Shoney's, I overheard someone talking to my mother about a fashion college. That's all it took. With the spirit of Designing Women, we packed up the truck and moved me to the big city of Atlanta so I could attend Bauder Fashion College. At that time, my dream was to design store windows or be a buyer for Macy's. Fashion and makeup have always been my lifelines, sometimes the only things that gave me the strength to put myself out there.

After college, I started in retail, terrified to even talk to customers. But that experience built confidence, and I worked my way up into management. Still, I wanted more. So, I swapped the retail floor for a corporate office. At just twenty-something, I was flying on the company's private jet to New York and thought I had reached the top. I actually thought every corporate job came with access to private jets. Bless my own heart, I learned quickly that's not the case. Pregnant with my second daughter, the company was sold, and my whole department was laid off. I was crushed.

But that setback pushed me higher. I gained experience by taking on projects no one else wanted, from hauling suitcases through malls to overseeing a 400-site signage conversion. I waddled into an interview eight months pregnant. I landed a role at one of the world's largest real estate companies, just as twelve cellular companies were merging into Cingular Wireless. They needed someone with experience in signage conversion, and there I was.

That was a turning point. Since then, I've led some of the world's largest brand conversion programs, often being told it couldn't be done. I've stumbled, been scared stiff, and still had to find the courage to stand tall and Bravely Lead.

You see, I didn't set out to be brave; I just refused to stop moving.

Life is never what we expect. It can be so much better, and at times, so much worse. It's not just a normal ride around the park; we're on the world's most spectacular roller coaster, full of ups, downs, twists, and turns. Some things you'll see coming, and others will surprise you like you're wearing a blindfold. It's all right, just hold on, do your best, and whatever happens, choose not to get off the ride.

You have to find your reason to keep going, and no two reasons are ever the same. They can change throughout your journey, and that's okay.

Mine started out simple: I just wanted to prove I was worthy.

After giving birth to two beautiful daughters, Victoria and Diana, my purpose shifted. I no longer wanted just to survive; I wanted to give them more. I wanted to give them confidence, laughter, and an example of a strong woman who could chase her dreams while holding her family close.

Have I done everything right? Not by any stretch of the imagination. I just try to make my mistakes with humor and humility. Mistakes are expected and welcomed, because they're the foundation of what makes us authentic.

So, here's the plain truth, y'all: this book is about finding your path, not the one some fancy expert on TV says you ought to take. I hope you'll keep going, even when your knees are knocking and your brain's hollering. Whatever challenge you're facing - whether it's career, life, or just getting out of bed on a hard day - I want you to find your courage, your confidence, and your funny bone. Because if I can do it, honey, so can you.

Bravely Leading

1

The Beginning

I bet I scared some of you with that title. Don't worry, I'm not going all the way back to the hot summer day when I made my grand entrance in August 1969. Instead, I'll start where things really began to take shape in college.

Every story has a beginning, but not all of them start where you expect. Mine begins with a suitcase packed for Atlanta: a small-town girl with big hair, a cheetah-print leotard, and way more dreams than dollars. I didn't know it yet, but that move would set the stage for everything that came after learning to speak up, show up, and lead well before I ever felt brave enough to.

But before any of that could happen, I had to learn one critical skill: how to harness fear in life and in interviews. Because let's be honest here, if you don't land the job, you'll never get your chance to Bravely Lead.

Heading Off to College

After high school, I was more than ready to be done with classrooms. My dream was to head straight to the mall and join my tribe of makeup-counter ladies. We would have put lipstick and mascara on the world. But my parents had other plans. They were set on my going to college.

Then one night at our local Shoney's, my mom struck up a conversation with a woman who told her about a fashion college in Atlanta. My ears perked up. Bauder was an education I could get behind. It mixed my love of *Designing Women* with real classes in fashion, makeup, and modeling. My brain started clicking. Moving to Atlanta, keeping my southern accent, studying fashion, maybe even designing window displays. Now that sounded like fun.

We looked into the school. It was expensive, but my parents found a way to make it happen. We loaded up the truck and headed to my aunt's house in Atlanta. I can still remember the weight of that August air as we headed up I-75. I'm not sure if it was the heaviness of the Southern humidity or our emotions. We tried to make small talk, but really, we were all fighting back tears. I sat between my parents, and my life was packed into the bed of the truck. I wasn't sure if I had made the biggest mistake or the best decision of my life.

I could write a whole book on those years, from the fun I had with my aunt and cousins to how the Bauder girls partied with the Georgia Tech guys, but we'd be here all day if I did. My cousins took me under their wings and made sure I was safe and well cared for. One would draw maps to help me get around the big city. That was well before cell phones and GPS, but I was never much of a map reader and quickly learned I was directionally challenged.

Eventually, my cousin figured out the secret: if he could help me navigate by using malls as landmarks, I'd always find my way. He'd say things like, "Do you know where Lenox Mall is?" and I'd proudly reply, "Of course!" Then he'd grin and say, "Good. Don't go that way." We'd laugh like it was the funniest thing we'd ever heard.

My other cousin and her husband took me to Georgia Tech football games, and we'd hang out at his fraternity house afterward. We'd play games, listen to bands, and make up our own lyrics. I can still hear "Darlia M." being sung instead of "Suzie Q." in that old CCR song.

Then there were the Georgia Tech guys brave enough to come to Bauder College, a school full of young women, to pass out party flyers. I don't know if they expected the girls not to show up or what, but we came in droves. The guys just stood along the wall like they were frozen in disbelief until their liquid courage finally kicked in.

Maybe I'll write that story someday, but this book is about *Bravely Leading*, so let's stay focused.

I didn't realize it then, but that trip from Tennessee to Georgia was my first act of brave leadership. I packed up fear, dreams, and enough hairspray to make it in the big city.

A Different Kind of Education

Bauder Fashion College was a world all its own, and I wouldn't trade a minute of it. Yes, we had classes in makeup and modeling, and even a course called "slimnastics," which was just a fancy word for aerobics. I loved it because I got to strut around in my cheetah leotard. Cheetah and leopard are still my favorite neutrals to this day.

But don't mistake my education for fluff and frills. We had solid classes in marketing, management, and even a Dale Carnegie course, *How to Win Friends and Influence People*, that could have been taught at Harvard and is still applicable today. The school's small size fostered close bonds between teachers and students, and there was an energy in that building that made you believe you could take on the world.

Bauder sat in Buckhead, tucked in the basement of Phipps Plaza, which meant we could walk to Lenox for lunch surrounded by fashion, passion, and everything that fueled our dreams. It wasn't unusual to see designers, models, and executives brushing shoulders with students learning to stand tall in their first pair of heels as they tried on their confidence.

Still, it wasn't all glitz and glamour. There were days I wondered if I was good enough and if my small-town sparkle could hold up in a city full of talent. Can you imagine being surrounded by some of the world's most beautiful students? But that doubt pushed me harder as I kept exploring what made me different and how I could possibly stand out in a sea of beauties. I worked on polishing my poise, grace, and humor. I held small stand-up comedy routines anytime I could get a gathering, trying to find ways to shine like the top of the Chrysler Building.

I thought I was doing everything perfectly until "sound-off." Now, although the school was in Atlanta, not all my classmates were Southerners. We had plenty of my darling friends from those Northern states as well. At the end of the first year, we had to stand up and say something we remembered from our first day at school. One student stood up and said, "Hello, my name is Darlia May, and I'm from Tennessee."

Now, that almost sounds like a compliment, but she said it in the most exaggerated Southern accent her little Northern voice could muster. It's funny to me now, but at the time I thought, *Oh, that's horrible!* And I started trying to modify my accent into something a little more palatable for all.

I pushed myself in my classes too, taking studying to a whole new level and focusing on everything I thought would make a difference when we left the comfort of the Bauder walls. I learned so much from making good first impressions, makeup for different occasions, projecting my voice, and putting on full fashion shows. We actually walked into stores, and they loaned us clothes for fashion shows!

In chemistry class, we had to burn different materials and recognize the fabric type by how it burned. Luckily, that's a skill I've never had to use after school.

However, the class that stands out the most was on interviewing skills. At first, it sounded simple, but think about it—where would any of us be if we never landed a job?

Interviewing is an art, and because of that class, I've landed numerous jobs over the years. And I'll shoot you straight here, I wasn't always the most qualified. Now, don't get confused. I've also interviewed and not gotten the job. But I learned something from every single one of those experiences, and each one helped me grow into the leader I was becoming.

Landing the Job - Apply Anyway

First things first. You have to apply. I know, you're probably thinking, "everybody knows that." But here's where men and women differ.

Women tend to read the job description 440 times, tearing themselves down until they've convinced themselves not to apply. They want to be sure they meet 100 percent of the requirements. Men, on the other hand, skim the description, decide they're the best candidate on the planet, and hit apply.

The truth is somewhere in the middle. If you meet 75 percent of the job requirements, apply. That's it. You can often bridge the gap with transferable skills from school, from work, or even from life.

I learned that lesson firsthand. I didn't meet every qualification for one of my first jobs, but I figured the worst they could say was no. So, I applied anyway.

A week later, I was sitting in a hotel lobby, not a red flag here, the interviewer was from out of state, but PSA: I said hotel lobby, not hotel room. I interviewed for the position, and by the end of that meeting, they offered me the job. That "why not" mindset has opened more doors than any fancy-pants degree ever could.

Interview Prep

Interviewing is nerve-racking for everyone, and it can be even harder if you wrestle with anxiety. Preparation can ease some of that.

Do your homework. Learn about the company, so you know what you're walking into.

Practice with a partner. Mock interviews help you prepare for both the expected and unexpected. I like to throw curveball questions such as "How many tennis balls fit in a limousine?" or "If you could be an animal, what would you be and why?" The point is to see how people think on their feet.

Skip the caffeine overload. Too much coffee plus adrenaline can equal a shaky disaster.

Power posing works. Before big moments, you can still find me in a hallway or bathroom striking my Superman or Wonder Woman stance. It calms your heart rate and can reset your confidence.

The Interview

It's showtime, the moment all that preparation comes to life. Whether it's in person, on the phone, or through a video screen, the same rules apply take a breath, believe you're worthy, and remember you're interviewing them just as much as they're interviewing you.

I still remember one of my early interviews when my hands were shaking so badly that I reached out to shake the interviewer's hand, and I knocked the picture right off his desk. All I could do was apologize through my nervous laughter. Then I stumbled through a few answers but stayed honest, even admitting, "I'm so nervous because I really want this job." The interviewer smiled, and the tension broke instantly. That moment taught me something powerful: people, no matter their title, connect with authenticity, not perfection.

So, if your nerves get the best of you, don't hide it. Acknowledge that you're nervous and explain why this opportunity matters to you. Tie it back to your homework about the company, or a cause you believe in. That moment of honesty can create a connection that sticks long after the interview is over.

Answer questions as best you can. If you're unsure, repeat the question to buy a little time. Before you leave, ask a few questions of your own, as people love to talk about themselves. If it's the hiring manager, ask how long they've been with the company or what they love about it. If it's HR, dig into benefits. Always thank them and confirm the following steps before you leave.

And remember you've already done the hard part. You showed up!

Follow Through

Welcome to the gray area. Everyone has an opinion about follow-up, so here's my advice.

Send a thank-you note. Keep it simple, personal, and genuine. A short message that references something specific from the conversation shows you were listening and that goes further than any formal script.

Respect the timeline you were given. Don't check in daily, like you're waiting for your favorite shoes to be on sale. Wait one to three days after the deadline before following up.

Be short and sweet. Ask if you can provide additional information. Then let it rest.

LinkedIn connections are case by case. If you felt a genuine connection, send the request. If not, let it go.

Early in my career, I missed out on a great opportunity because I assumed silence meant rejection. Months later, the manager told me they had waited to see who followed up, and I hadn't. Lesson learned: professionalism doesn't end when the interview does.

Following through isn't about pestering; it's about presence. It shows confidence, attention to detail, and respect: three qualities that never go unnoticed and always stand out when you're Bravely Leading.

Negotiation

Congratulations, you've been offered the job. Now comes the part that makes many people squirm like a worm on hot Georgia asphalt: the dreaded negotiation.

Most women accept the first number offered. Men do a little better, but both sides often leave money on the table. Negotiation should be about facts, not feelings. Do your homework on salary ranges, work-life balance, and expectations. If the offer is fair and in line with your experience, it's okay to say yes. But it never hurts to ask for a day or two to think it over.

As a woman executive, I've been on both sides of the table, and I'll be honest, I never liked it. But one story stays with me. Years ago, a woman with a strong reputation told me her salary requirement. I knew she was underpricing herself. Most people would have happily paid her what she asked. I couldn't do it.

I looked at her and said, "Welcome to the team, but I can't pay you what you're asking. I need you to raise that number."

When I offered her more, she cried. It was one of the most touching moments of my career. She became a loyal and dedicated employee for years.

That day taught me something I'll never forget when you recognize someone's value and choose to pay them like you mean it, you don't just hire talent. You inspire loyalty. And that, right there, is what *Bravely Leading* looks like. And a HELL of a motivator!

Lessons Learned from Chapter One

If you meet 75 percent of the job requirements, **apply anyway.** The worst they can say is *no*, and sometimes that "no" is what pushes you to the right "yes".

Preparation builds confidence. The more you practice, the less space fear has to run the show.

Nerves aren't a weakness. When you're honest about them, when you own up to them, they can turn strangers into friends and awkwardness into authenticity.

Follow through without becoming a pest. People remember confidence and kindness, not the person who checks in every day, like they're waiting on biscuits to rise.

Negotiate your worth. You're more valuable than you think, and courage at the table can change your entire future.

Every opportunity, big or small, is a lesson in leading yourself first. That's how you build courage, one small step at a time, before you're ever called to *Bravely Lead*.

2

Early Career

When I look back on my early career, it fills my heart with pure joy. The kind that makes you sing in the car, show up early because you want to, not because someone is watching. It's not the polished kind that comes from shiny shoes and fancy job titles, but the simple kind that starts long before a paycheck ever arrives. Those were the years of discovery, where imagination was my boss and curiosity was my co-worker.

And I'm not just talking about the positions we hold after finishing school. If you start there, you've already missed the first lessons, the ones hidden in childhood work and play. My first jobs didn't come with paychecks, and truthfully, yours shouldn't either. The things that fuel your soul are the things you would do even if you never made a dime.

Looking back now, I realize that courage doesn't start with a title: it starts with joy, the kind that keeps you creating, dreaming, and showing up even when no one's watching.

Childhood Joys

As a little girl, I performed for anyone who would watch. I sang, I danced, and even made-up songs myself. I still remember one called

"Apple Pie in the Sky." It never made the charts, but for a six-year-old belting it out in the driveway to an audience of stuffed animals and dolls, it was pure satisfaction. I am pretty confident that old teddy bear will be a fan for life.

And when I wasn't performing, I was creating worlds on paper. I wrote chapter books filled with drama and spelling errors. Thank goodness typewriters didn't have spellcheck, or I might never have finished that story about Becky sneaking lipstick. At the time, it was just play, but looking back, I know those were passions that pointed me toward my purpose.

Those early passions shaped my love for storytelling, connection, and creativity. They are the same skills I use today when I stand on a stage or lead a team through change. When you bring pieces of your childhood joy into adulthood, life feels easier, lighter, and full of energy. I believe that is God's way of reminding us of where our true purpose begins and continually nudging us toward our calling in simple, subtle ways.

When you feel stuck or out of sync with your joy, pause and look back on your childhood. Those magical moments are clues, gentle reminders of who you are and where your happiness begins.

Learning Beside My Dad

Some of my earliest lessons came from working with my dad. Calling him incredible would be an understatement. He was a fireman, eventually Fire Chief, a contractor, and a city council member. But his true passion was creation. He built homes, furniture, and people's confidence with the same care and craftsmanship.

From the time I could walk, he brought me along. I drove nails, kept records, and even "helped" when I was only four and barely useful. My brother and I helped my parents finish a basement, and I was so little that he had to stick me in the wheelbarrow and let me ride just to move me out of the way. But I rode on top of that dirt like a fairytale princess in a parade. My brother had a great imagination, too, so it might have been work, but he always found ways to make it fun.

My favorite part was riding into town with my dad for store visits. He always introduced me as the boss in such a way that I one hundred percent believed I was the boss, no question. I'd carry a pen and paper, make notes, and help choose materials.

It never once crossed my mind, until writing this book, that my dad could have done those trips faster without me. But instead, he let me feel like I had conquered the world. He taught me that real leaders don't just build things, they build confidence in others. He led through patience, trust, and quiet strength, long before I ever knew that's what leadership looked like. I had the opportunity to witness it firsthand.

Those moments didn't just shape me into the leader I became. They showed me that creation isn't about control; it's about care.

Strong Female Role Models

A Mother Who Taught with Imagination

My mother was a schoolteacher, and she didn't turn it off at home. We played school constantly. I'm sure part of it was her trying to help me learn so I wouldn't struggle as much, but she made it fun.

One day, we were playing school, and I was the teacher while she played the student. She told me if I didn't stop bossing her around, she'd tell her mama, and then she added, "She'll come here and that will really scare you." I looked at her, confused, and said, "Why?" She said, "Because she's dead!"

Now, who says that to a child? Well, we do in the South. We love a good story, a little exaggeration, and a touch of the dramatic. If that isn't good old-fashioned Southern flair, I don't know what is.

My Mom had a way of mixing humor, love, and lessons so you never quite knew which one you were getting. She also gave me the freedom to create, to explore, to dream without limits. If I wanted to write a chapter book before I could even spell, she got me a typewriter. If I wanted to get on stage and dance with a band at the mall, she let me march right up and ask.

I guess she probably should have stopped me that time, as I got up there and did the swim and the monkey to Christian music right in the center of the Cleveland Mall.

Asking to do unheard-of things feels easy when you're a child, because the world hasn't yet told you what's impossible. My mother made sure that confidence stayed with me long after childhood ended. She showed me that learning isn't just about rules and books. It's about curiosity, courage, and believing you belong wherever you choose to stand.

Grace, Grit, and Lipstick

In high school, I had two jobs that paid. My first job was with a friend's mother, who just so happened to be a successful career woman in my town, and at that time, there weren't many of those. Now, I don't know if she really had any official duties for me, but she certainly brought me into her circle. She let me work with her in the studio and, on some days, even paid me to take my friend to the lake.

You'd think a paid day at the lake with a friend would have been my favorite part of the job, but honey, it wasn't. Watching this lady in action from the office to the country club was something to see. She could work a room and any crowd we encountered.

"Honey" will always be her word, I can't think of her without hearing it in her familiar drawl. It was more than a word; it was the essence of who she was. She had a talent to make it drip with sweetness or sting with sharpness, and either way, people listened. She taught me that you can be your authentic Southern self while still commanding respect. Those lunches were my first lessons in thriving in a male-dominated world, well before I knew how important that would be in my career.

The second job was at a makeup counter in a hair salon. I thought it would be fun, but it taught me the magic of helping people feel confident. Watching women walk in hiding from the world and walk out with their heads held high was powerful.

The day the bride chose me to do her wedding makeup nearly sent me into panic mode, but it turned out beautifully. I almost declined since I was the newest makeup artist in the salon. She knew that but told me how impressed she'd been with my work. So, I approached that opportunity like it was brain surgery, honey. The last thing I wanted was to send a bride down the aisle looking like the Bride of Frankenstein. I still remember her smile when she looked in the mirror and saw her natural beauty enhanced through my artistry. That moment taught me to step up when the pressure is on and trust my instincts, even when my hands are shaking.

Both women showed me something I still carry today: that confidence can be both graceful and bold, and that lifting others up is one of the purest forms of leadership. Those early jobs taught me that leadership doesn't always start with a title; sometimes it begins behind a makeup counter or in the presence of a woman who makes "honey" sound like both a blessing and a challenge.

The Late-Blooming Trailblazer

One of the strongest female role models in my life came a little later, when I moved to Atlanta for college and lived with my **Aunt Betty**. She had just finished law school in her fifties. Now that's a strong female role model, teaching me you're never too old to follow your dreams. She said the younger students took everything so seriously and were scared to death, but she was just excited to be out of the house.

She was one of the best roommates ever. I was a busy college student, and she was launching her new career at the Securities and Exchange Commission. We both had full schedules but always made time for dinner together once a week. She helped me adjust to big-city life and took me to plays at the Alliance Theatre. We gave each other freedom, maybe a little too much at times.

Once, I left a note on the fridge saying I was going to Florida with a friend. When I didn't come home that night, Aunt Betty panicked, thinking it was an old note from the week before, and called my parents in a frenzy. Luckily, they knew exactly where I was. It was the '80s, pre-cell phones, when "tracking someone down" meant calling everyone they might know.

Our most fun memory came during an Atlanta "snowstorm," which really meant we were iced in. We watched television, sang every commercial, and talked about everything under the sun. Aunt Betty made her famous chili and set it outside to keep it cold. That worked perfectly until she tried to bring it back in; the ice won, and she did a full-on split.

After a week of being stuck inside, I couldn't take it anymore. I decided the most important thing I could do was check the mail. I know, it sounds ridiculous, if you can't get down the driveway, there's probably not much mail to get. But out I went, sliding all the way down the yard until I grabbed a tree to stop me. That's exactly where my parents found me, hanging on for dear life, as they pulled into the driveway after their treacherous drive from Tennessee.

Those days with Aunt Betty taught me that independence doesn't mean isolation. You can chase your dreams, laugh at your missteps or slippery steps, and still make time for the people who keep you grounded.

The Women Who Raised My Confidence

I was lucky to grow up surrounded by many strong, spirited women who each taught me something different about life, love, and laughter. They weren't just family; they were living lessons in confidence and grace.

The Elegant Adventurer

My **Nana** was the one who showed me how to travel with purpose and in style. I kept my suitcase packed so I'd always be ready whenever she wanted to head to Atlanta. On Saturday nights, I'd spend the night at her house, watching *The Carol Burnett Show* before church the next morning. She dressed impeccably, always with a hat, lipstick, and just the right amount of attitude.

When my Papaw was driving and she didn't like how he handled the road, she'd sigh and say, "Well, shit, Milford," in that way only a Southern woman can make a curse word sound charming. If the grandkids in the backseat started acting up, she'd just swing her hand back without even looking. I was her little traveling buddy, so I somehow managed to dodge the swats, but the memory of those car rides still makes me laugh. Especially how heavy her foot was on the gas pedal at times.

From Nana, I learned that confidence isn't about having everything figured out. It's about showing up with curiosity, grace, and a little sparkle in your step, hat and all.

The Joyful Competitor

My **Mamaw** taught me the importance of loving yourself, flaws and all. She could find joy in the smallest things, and she had this nervous laugh that could light up an entire room. When the grandkids came over, she'd race us around the house, and she'd win every time. I'm still not sure if she was really that fast or if we were laughing too hard to run straight. I can still hear her squealing as she rounded the corner, pure delight in her voice.

She loved telling stories about growing up on the farm and about her animals, which she treated like family. She was a vegetarian, and to this day, none of us know if it was because of her Seventh-day Adventist faith or because she simply couldn't bear to eat her best friends. Either way, she lived with a gentle strength and a big laugh.

From Mamaw, I learned that mistakes aren't failures; they're proof that you're trying. And that laughter, especially in chaos, is sometimes the bravest sound you can make.

The Lasting Light

There was **Aunt Beryl**, my great-aunt who lived to be over one hundred years old. When I was little, she babysat me and told endless stories about her days working in a clothing store. Her eyes would light up as she described helping women find the perfect dress, the one that made them stand taller and smile bigger. She used to call me her *little diamond*, and maybe that's why I grew up believing I was meant to shine perfectly polished or not, but precious just the same.

When I saw her at her hundredth birthday celebration, she told me she wished I lived closer so she could babysit my daughter. And I knew she meant it. Even at one hundred, she still carried that same spark of love, humor, and confidence that had defined her whole life.

The Gentle Encourager

And then there was **Aunt Dale**, who had two daughters, one of them just a week younger than me, so I was at her house a lot growing up. Every year, she let us dye Easter eggs in her kitchen. We stained her countertops year after year, and she never seemed to care, as long as we were laughing and having fun.

She was also the best hair washer in the world. She'd lay us across her kitchen counter and wash our hair in the sink, her warm hands massaging away the day. Even now, as an adult, I've had moments when I just wanted to lie on her counter again and let her wash my hair not just for the warm water, but for the laughter and the love that came with it. It felt like therapy before I ever knew what therapy was.

The Lesson in Their Legacy

Looking back, I realize these women were some of my first leadership teachers. They never gave lectures about bravery or self-worth;

they just lived it beautifully. They showed me that I could do anything I set my mind to, as long as my self-confidence was aligned.

From them, I learned that strength doesn't have to be loud, beauty doesn't have to be perfect, and laughter can get you through almost anything. Let's be honest here, there are times in life where laughter is what keeps us going. They taught me that grace can coexist with grit, and that love, the real, everyday kind, is often found in the smallest moments: a shared story, a warm sink, or a road trip that starts with "Well, shit, Milford."

Early Retail Adventures

After college, I managed a booth in the mall selling sports paraphernalia. I didn't care a thing about sports, but I studied the newspaper every morning like I was prepping for a final exam. I wanted to keep up with customers and sounded like I knew what I was talking about. Sales came naturally, but leadership brought a few surprises and a few stories I'll never forget.

The first surprise was firing my first employee. He was lazy, often late, and eventually had to go. I thought I was prepared, but I wasn't. It never crossed my mind that he would start screaming in the middle of the mall, loud enough to wake the dead, or at least for security to come running and escort his butt out of there. He showed back up in the parking lot later that evening and busted out my car's windows, which thankfully happened only once in my career. That day, I learned leadership doesn't always come with applause. Sometimes it simply comes with glass on the ground, or, for that matter, on the ceiling.

The second surprise was theft. Shirts and hats kept disappearing, and we couldn't figure out how. Inventory checks indicated it was happening overnight, after closing and before opening, so I worked with mall security. They found a great little hideout on the roof where they had the sports booth in perfect eyeshot for overnight viewing. Sure enough, the janitorial staff was fishing merchandise through a gap in the caulk like they were reeling in a catfish. Fixing the caulk fixed the problem.

Then there was the time I was so sick I could barely stand, but the kiosk had to open or we'd be fined. I dragged myself to the mall, unlocked the store, and basically laid down on the floor behind the counter. If a customer came up, I hauled myself up enough for them to see me over the counter and did my best to sell through a fog. My parents came with a drink and stayed until someone could cover my shift. I didn't sell a thing that day; I'm guessing no one wanted to buy anything from a zombie on the floor, but I did what had to be done. Looking back, it was ridiculous and brave in equal measure.

I also worked in a few retail stores, and those gigs taught me styling, honesty, and personal courage. At Casual Corner, I loved finding the best-looking outfits for every client who walked in. Women would search me out because they trusted I wouldn't tell them something looked good if it didn't. I wouldn't straight-up insult anyone, but I'd always offer an alternative that fits their style. Everyone left with something that elevated their look and their confidence.

Shoplifters were another part of retail education. If it were a random shopper, I'd sometimes be bold and ask how they planned to pay for the scarf tucked into their bag. I might not do that today, but back then I was young, brave, and maybe a little naïve about risk. Once, the pros hit a string of stores and crawled on their bellies, cutting security chains and making off with merchandise. I waited for them to clear my store and then called mall security. They caught them, and I had to identify them from a distance. It wasn't the type of excitement I expected that day, but it taught me more about balancing safety and confidence than any security conference ever could.

Those early lessons taught me that leadership isn't about knowing everything; it's about staying calm, involving others, and solving problems together. Every challenge, even the messy ones, became a little brick in the foundation of the leader I was becoming, one hard lesson at a time.

Outgrowing the Work

I stayed in retail for several years, moving from one role to another, always trying to convince myself that the next promotion or pay raise would make it better. And for a little while, it did. I was good at what I did. I loved the customers, the people, and the art of turning chaos into calm. But no matter how much I smiled or how shiny my title got, that little spark inside me started to fade.

Eventually, I stepped away, thinking the problem was the long hours and the weekends that stole time from my family. But looking back, the misery wasn't about hours. It was about being unfulfilled. I wanted more than folding blouses and meeting sales goals. I wanted to build something, lead something, leave a mark that lasted longer than this season's fashion trend.

The day I realized I couldn't fake it anymore was a Sunday morning. I was sitting on my kitchen's white and black checkered floor in my pajamas, coffee gone cold beside me, crying because I didn't want to go to work. Not because of the people or the paycheck, but because I couldn't stand one more day of pretending I was happy. My husband at the time thought I was losing it, but deep down, I knew I was losing myself. Somewhere between early ambition and adult responsibility, I had stopped growing. I had stopped reaching for my dreams in the stars, and I knew they were still out there waiting for me.

That realization scared me, not because I was failing, but because I wasn't stretching. I missed learning. I missed creating. I missed the part of me that believed there was something more out there.

It took me a long time to understand that outgrowing something doesn't mean you failed at it. It means you've taken everything it has to offer. You've learned the lessons, collected the wisdom, and now you're being nudged toward something new.

That moment on the kitchen floor was the quiet before the next leap. I didn't know it yet, but I was giving myself permission to change paths. I didn't need my husband to understand or even back me in my decision. I didn't need my boss or anyone else to fully understand. I just needed to trust in myself and do what inside I knew needed to be done. That small act of bravery, choosing growth over comfort, would set the stage for everything that came next.

Lessons Learned from Chapter Two

Lead through care. Leadership isn't about control; it's about lifting others and helping them grow, just like my dad taught me.

Find joy in learning. My mom showed me that curiosity and imagination make every lesson stick — even the ones that come with laughter and a little drama.

Dream beyond limits. Aunt Betty reminded me that it's never too late to chase a dream or start something new. Courage has no expiration date.

Stay curious and creative. Sometimes the best ideas come from play, freedom, and the confidence to ask for what feels impossible.

Know when to move on. Growth means outgrowing old paths, even when they once felt right.

Live with laughter and grace. My Nana, Mamaw, Aunt Beryl, and Aunt Dale taught me that confidence shines brighter when paired with kindness, humor, and love. The way you carry yourself, with a smile, a sparkle, and maybe a little sass, can be its own kind of leadership.

You don't need anyone's permission to redefine your path. This is your life, and you get to decide when it's time to turn the page.

The joy that starts in childhood doesn't disappear; it quietly waits for you to remember. And when you do, that joy becomes the fuel that carries you into every brave step ahead.

3

Welcome to Corporate!

Well, I did it. I finally mustered the courage to quit a job that no longer fulfilled me and took the next scary step toward something bigger. It was time to move from the retail floor to a corporate office, going from selling to strategy, and from name tags to business cards.

Now, let's not get too excited. My first position was in customer service, working in the order fulfillment department at Wolf Camera. It wasn't exactly the glamorous corner office with a secretary or butler I had pictured, but it was a start and beat the heck out of folding sweaters. I showed up every day ready to learn. We even spent one day a week in the warehouse packing and shipping orders, and I loved it. That experience gave me a behind-the-scenes view of how things really worked, where the bottlenecks were, how processes could be improved, and why paying attention to details mattered.

The customer service job was fine for getting my foot in the door, but I knew I wanted more. Creativity has always been my north star, so I found ways to collaborate with advertising, marketing, and store design. Wolf Camera was small enough, and the leaders were open enough that you could move around and gain experience. I took every chance available to learn something new, even when it wasn't part of my job description.

Looking back, it's still one of my favorite roles. We worked hard, and we laughed harder. Some of my lifelong friendships were formed in those cubicles, and the flexibility that the company gave me built a foundation for how I lead my teams today with trust, fun, and the freedom to grow.

Finding My Fit

When the store design team at Wolf Camera learned about my degree in merchandising and my passion for design, they transferred me to their department as soon as an opening came up. I was excited beyond words to transition out of customer service and into a role that felt more aligned with my desire to create. There was some nervousness mixed in with that excitement, since the team consisted of a wide range of characters. They were smart, loud, opinionated, and all quite unique. I tried to silence the fear of not being ready. Deep down, I knew that timing and flexibility had always played a big part in my career development, and that the time was now.

One of my first assignments was setting up scrapbooking departments inside key stores. Now, I've always loved fashion and design, but crafts? Not so much. Still, I jumped in with both feet. I lugged suitcases through malls, set up tables in front of camera stores, and taught customers how to scrapbook. It built relationships and gave people a creative space to share their family stories. Even my coworkers got involved, creating pages that ended up in my example book. I can still picture those slightly over-accessorized layouts of pets and holidays; each one made with so much heart.

That role also gave me my first taste of business travel. On one trip to Savannah, we scheduled ourselves so tightly that we carved out exactly two hours to go to the beach. That little trick of finding joy even in a packed schedule has stayed with me throughout my career. It taught me that the best work comes when you leave space for a bit of life in between the deadlines, meetings, and flights. The more years

I've led teams, the more I've come to realize that both creativity and people need breathing room. When I push through weeks packed with back-to-back meetings, those are never the weeks I do my best work.

Lessons and Lobster Tails

Once the scrapbook push was complete, I shifted back into store design. Our team worked closely with construction crews on branding, merchandise placement, and fixtures. We even took a class at Georgia Tech to learn how to read construction drawings. That class was a game-changer and turned me into a lifelong learner.

One of my most exciting projects was building flagship stores in New York City. We flew back and forth from Atlanta, often on the company's private jet. I was a young mom in my twenties and thought I had reached the top of the world. Each seat had its own entertainment system, unheard of at the time, and we could even request the food we wanted on board. I was so young I thought all corporate jobs came with private jet rides, but I still pinched myself just to make sure I wasn't dreaming. During those flights, I'd pretend to watch a movie, but really I was practicing what I'd say when we landed, how I'd handle things if the stores didn't look right, and what clever comment I could make at dinner.

On one of those trips, we had dinner in Little Italy with a few VPs. We sat at a large table in the center of the restaurant, surrounded by waiters who all looked like professional models. I ordered pasta with lobster, not realizing it would arrive in its shell. Trying to keep my composure in front of the VPs and all those beautiful people, I wrestled with it until the lobster flew out and landed squarely on top of my head, pasta sauce and all. Without missing a beat, one of the VPs grinned and said, "We can dress her up, but we can't take her out." Everyone burst out laughing, thankfully with me, not at me. At that moment, I knew I had found my crew.

That dinner became more than just a funny story. It reminded me that confidence isn't about being flawless; it's about laughing, learning, and showing up anyway. Each project, each class, and yes, even each flying lobster, taught me to carry myself with humor and humility, two ingredients that would serve me well for the rest of my career.

As I always say, mistakes will happen, my friends, and you should learn to laugh at yourself, no matter what your title is. In fact, the bigger the title, the better. When we learn to laugh at ourselves, we give comfort to others and create space for them to be their authentic selves, too.

The Pre-Christmas Party Fiasco

It was the day of our office Christmas party, and I was feeling good, really good. I had lost some weight and was wearing this olive-green suit with a fitted jacket, pleated skirt, and heels. Let's be honest, I wasn't just excited about the party; I was excited about how I looked and felt.

I was sitting up straight at my desk, focused on an email, when out of nowhere, one of my prankster coworkers decided it was the perfect time for a laugh. She snuck up behind me, hit the lever on my chair, and catapulted me forward like a slingshot. Before I could even think, I jumped up, spun around, and punched her square in the arm, right there in the middle of the office.

Now here's the kicker: she wasn't just a coworker. She was my **boss**.

We both froze for a second, then scurried back to our cubicles. A few seconds later, I saw her pick up her phone. I yelled, "You better not be calling your mom!" as I was already dialing mine. I can still hear my dad in the background saying, "She hit her boss? Does she still have a job?"

A few minutes later, I got an email from her, typed with only the fingers on her right hand, pretending her left arm was useless. That did it. We laughed so hard we couldn't catch our breath. But we both decided we should probably get ahead of the story and go straight to our VP before anyone else did.

We walked into her office and said, "We had a little... situation." Our VP looked up from her desk, clearly bracing herself, and we told her we'd had a "fistfight in the middle of the floor." She raised one eyebrow, sighed, and said, "Ladies, what have we learned from this story?" Without missing a beat, my boss said, "That Darlia has a mean right hook." We all burst out in laughter.

The next day, my boss, still one of my best friends to this day, helped me pack for a move. She showed up wearing a fake sling on her left arm. We laughed so hard we couldn't get a single box taped.

Now, hear me out. I am in no way recommending that you hit your boss or anyone else at work. But I will say this: **find your lifetime work friends who help you laugh through the chaos and find the silver lining in everything you do.**

Following The Signs

We finished those stores and countless other projects. Our team worked hard but always found ways to have fun; heck, we even went skiing through the office in file folder boxes. Deadlines were met, creativity flowed, and for the first time, I truly felt like I was part of something bigger than myself.

Then came the project that changed everything. Wolf Camera had just bought Fox Photo, a company with more than four hundred locations, and someone needed to manage the signage conversion. No one had the time or the experience, so I volunteered. I knew I wasn't the most qualified, but everyone else had a specialty: construction, design, or merchandising, and I was still trying to find mine. So as my heart pounded to the point I could hear it in my ears, my hand shot up before my brain had a chance to catch up and talk me out of it. If I had known then all the complexities involved with signage, there's no way I would have thrown my hat in the mix. Thank goodness for that naivety and fast hands.

That single decision shaped the rest of my career. I soaked up everything I could about how signs were made, installed, and how much detail went into getting them right. I worked with vendors, documented processes, and built partnerships that still stand strong today. I got into the nitty-gritty of raw materials, learning which lighting paired with which vinyl to shine the perfect color at night. In my mind, I was pairing them like fine wine with food. Some combinations clashed, but when you got it right, the result was magic.

The project was demanding, fast-paced, and full of unknowns, but I loved every insane minute of it. I still remember all the companies and the personnel names I worked with on that program. Probably because I tracked every detail so closely and knew they were teaching me as much as following my lead. There was something deeply satisfying about taking something complex and turning it into a clear, visible message that represented an entire brand.

I didn't know it then, but those signs weren't just guiding customers. They were guiding me, lighting the path toward a career that would shape three decades of my life and teach me lessons I now share through my work today.

A Little Backseat Wisdom

When I was pregnant with my second daughter, mornings often started with me taking my oldest to preschool. I always tried to make our time together fun by singing, playing games, and doing whatever I could to keep her entertained. As a working mom, I've always believed it's the quality of the time you spend, not the quantity, that matters most.

One morning, we were a bit rushed but packed up with our usual juice boxes and snacks. I didn't want the chaos of the morning to spill over into her day, so I decided to lighten the mood with our usual car singing. This time, I added a little Hokey Pokey to the mix. I had one hand on the wheel and one in the air, shaking it all about, when my three-year-old suddenly gave me the most serious look and said, "Now, Mom, you just need to keep both your hands on the wheel."

That moment cracked me up, but it also reminded me that sometimes the best wisdom comes from the backseat. Even at three years old, she had a way of grounding me and reminding me that balance matters, whether it's between work and home or hands and steering wheels.

We all need to have fun and relax, but every great project manager knows: safety first.

The Layoff

Life was good. Work was fulfilling, I was pregnant with my second daughter, and I truly thought I'd be with this company forever; it felt like home. We were in the office laughing and working as only this department could. The room was buzzing with the usual chatter, and tasks were being completed no differently than any other day, when everything changed.

We were brought into a conference room and told that Wolf Camera had been bought. Departments were being merged, and store design was being eliminated. If you're closing stores, you don't need new ones. Then we were called into human resources one at a time to hear the details of our terminations.

I remember leaning against the wall, waiting for my name to be called. It was a strange mix of standing and trying not to pass out. Had the wall not been there, I might have been on the floor. I stood there in my professional maternity clothes, feeling like a failure and grieving as if someone had died. I suppose something did die that day. My innocence in believing that doing your best always guarantees a positive outcome.

When I heard my name, my unborn daughter and I slowly walked into the room. The words hung in the air, heavy and unreal. I stared at the faces around the table, searching for some sign that I'd misunderstood. But I hadn't. Pregnant, emotional, and the sole breadwinner for my family, I crumbled. I sobbed uncontrollably.

When I got home, I couldn't even say the word "laid off." I told my family I'd been fired because, somehow, that felt easier to explain. What I didn't have the words for then was how lost I felt, not just professionally, but personally. So much of my identity had been wrapped up in doing well, providing, and proving myself.

With time and perspective, I came to understand that it wasn't personal. It was business. But at that moment, it felt deeply personal. I had given my all, and still, it wasn't enough to keep the ground steady beneath me.

That day taught me one of the hardest lessons of leadership: even when you pour your heart into the work, things will happen that are beyond your control. It took years to see it, but that ending was really just a new beginning.

Lessons Learned from Chapter Three

Be a lifetime learner. Every skill you pick up along the way becomes part of your foundation, even when it doesn't seem connected at first.

Keep laughter close. Hard work matters, but joy keeps you moving through the long stretches and the hard seasons.

Lead with both professionalism and heart. Speak up, listen well, and build authentic connections with people at every level.

Say yes to the work no one else wants. Those are the assignments that teach you the most and set you apart from the crowd.

Accept what you can't control. Layoffs, setbacks, and heartbreak will happen—but they don't define you. What defines you is what you do next.

Every chapter, even the painful ones, holds a lesson. Some will make you laugh, some will make you cry, but all of them are shaping you into the leader you were meant to become.

Remember to have fun. Careers are long. You need more laughter than tears to stay balanced and productive; if not, you'll burn yourself too fast - like bacon in a skillet.

Find your people. The ones who challenge you, cheer for you, and help you find the humor in even your wildest workdays - even when things are crazier than a fox in a hen house.

4

The Opportunity

The next few days were full of a cloudy haze of mixed emotions. There was happiness in waking up at a slower pace, holding my daughter a little longer in the mornings, and finding extra time for playing. Those sweet moments were mixed with a quiet panic that never left the back of my mind. I kept running the numbers in my head: how long we could make it on savings, which bills we could postpone, and how much formula and diapers cost. I'd find myself smiling at my daughter while silently calculating how long we could go before the next paycheck.

My husband and I made a pact: whoever found a job first would go back to work, and the other would stay home with the kids. Deep down, I already knew it would be me. That knowledge came with its own complicated emotions of pride, guilt, determination, and a good dose of fear. I'd always been the doer, the fixer, the one who made things happen. But now, with a baby on the way and no steady income, even my faith in "everything works out" was being tested.

I tried to stay busy, to keep my mind off the uncertainty. At night, I'd lie awake listening to the hum of the baby monitor and the stillness of the house, wondering how we'd make ends meet. It wasn't just the money. It was identity, the fear of becoming invisible, of being "the woman who used to have a career." I didn't know it yet, but that quiet fear was about to become fuel.

Then one day, out of the clear blue sky, the phone call came that changed everything. One of my former VPs told me that Jones Lang LaSalle, one of the largest real estate companies in the world, was hiring project managers with experience in signage conversion. She thought I should apply.

Now, I knew I had the experience. But that setback pushed me higher. I'd built up real, hard-earned experience just by saying yes when everyone else said no, taking on everything from hauling suitcases through malls to wrangling a 400-site signage conversion, but interviewing with a company that big? That felt intimidating. Still, I mustered up my nerve to pick up the phone while holding my oldest daughter's hand and hoping she would be relatively quiet during the call. The easy part was scheduling the interview. The hard part was walking—or, in my case at the time, waddling into that interview very pregnant and intimidated.

The Interview

I prepared as if it were a final exam. I had never called myself a project manager before, but once I understood the role, I realized I had been doing it for years. A project manager plans, organizes, and directs projects from start to finish. They need flexibility and just enough foresight to dodge pitfalls.

And yes, you better believe I went shopping. Confidence sometimes starts with what you put on and the psychology of how it makes you feel. I'll never forget that navy-blue maternity pantsuit. It was flattering, but there was no hiding that belly I hadn't yet learned to love. Still, it made me feel like a million bucks.

That morning, I kissed my oldest daughter, touched my belly for my youngest, and made them a promise. I promised to do my best to be a role model, to show them that a woman can pave her own way in a career and still be a loving mother. I promised I would be brave, even when I was scared. I knew I'd be a bit different from the cooking-and-cleaning type. I wanted to show them there's so much more to being a woman, because they deserved so much more.

On my way to the interview, I slid my seat back in the car to make room for my belly and tried to find the most comfortable position possible. After a few wrong turns and more luck than reading comprehension, I managed to navigate the parking garage and find a spot. I took a deep breath, smoothed my jacket, and slowly got out of the car, approaching the building as if it were a giant haunted house.

I opened the door, and the sound of my heels clanked across the marble lobby floor. We made our way up the elevator, and when the doors opened, the beauty of the space took my breath away with the dark mahogany panels and gleaming marble. It was the fanciest office I had ever entered, and I was actually there for an interview.

I sat tall in the lobby, smiling at everyone who walked by. When they called my name, I whispered to myself, "Showtime."

The man interviewing me was kind and dynamic, the kind of leader who made you feel seen. He asked thoughtful questions and listened closely. When I told him I'd already managed a 450 site signage conversion, he raised his eyebrows and smiled. "That's more experience than all of us," he said. For the first time in weeks, I felt the knot in my chest begin to loosen.

We even talked openly about my pregnancy and maternity leave with no awkward pauses, no side glances, just an honest conversation about what I could bring to the team. By the end of the interview, he shook my hand and said, "We look forward to having you join us."

When I walked out with the offer in hand, I stood in the lobby for a moment, stunned. My reflection in the marble floor looked like a woman I hadn't seen in a while capable, confident, and brave. I was sure glad I hadn't talked myself out of applying.

Jumping In

The program was massive and moved fast. Twelve companies were merging into one brand, Cingular Wireless, which later became AT&T. I was thrilled to be on the team. Just like the song from *Smokey and the Bandit*, "We had a long way to go and a short time to get there," and we certainly did what they said couldn't be done. That line became one of my themes throughout the rest of my career.

It was my first taste of working on a truly national scale, and I was determined to prove myself. On one of my first site walks, the client mentioned how great it would be if interior and exterior surveys could be combined. That night, I went home, sketched out a sample floor plan, and brought it back the next day. He was floored. That little bit of initiative taught me that truly listening (not just eavesdropping!) and jumping in to help would be one of my biggest strengths as a project manager.

Our team eventually moved from the fancy Buckhead office into a client call center. The décor was less impressive, but communication thrived with everyone under one roof. We became a true team of problem solvers, road warriors, and, at times, comic relief for one another. I worked right up until my daughter was born, including one too-bumpy flight where my client turned to me and said, "You're a trouper."

The "trouper" persona fit me well, but what most people didn't know was that getting to the office each day took a lot of determination and a Big Gulp cup from the gas station. Not because I loved soda, but because pregnancy nausea could strike at any moment. One day, I was driving a few team members to lunch when someone casually reached for my Big Gulp. I shouted "No, don't touch that!" but it was too late. It was hilarious and disgusting at the same time, and the story became an instant team legend.

That wild season taught me that leadership isn't about being perfect; it's about showing up anyway. Whether sketching plans at midnight or cracking up with a Big Gulp in hand, I figured out that if you show up with humor and hustle, folks will follow you just about any-where.

Balancing Babies and Work

Six weeks later, I returned from maternity leave with my heart split in two - wanting to be at work but aching to stay home. It wasn't easy, but I kept my promise to my daughters and pushed forward, deter-mined to show them that love and ambition can coexist.

Then came a steelworkers' strike in the Northeast. It delayed sign production and gave me my first crash course in unions. There were letters, negotiations, and sleepless nights, but we figured it out. That was the beauty of that season: no matter the obstacle, we found a way through.

Our team bonded through chaos. Sometimes the client lists sent us to empty fields labeled 'cows' or 'pigs' instead of stores. We joked about slapping a sign on a pig just to check it off the list. We were young, working hard, and doing our best to keep things light.

Not every day was light, though. One morning, I came in to find my desk rearranged. Exhausted, I sent a dramatic all-team email call-ing out "whoever sat at my desk." A friend jokingly replied, explaining that he'd sat there to upgrade my equipment. It was brilliant, and I felt ridiculous. Looking back, I laugh, but that day taught me how easy it is to overreact under stress.

Motherhood, deadlines, and leadership were all colliding, and I was still learning the art of balance and how to give grace to others and to myself. That lesson has stayed with me ever since: sometimes the most essential leadership skill isn't decision-making or delegation; it's knowing when to pause, breathe, and laugh at yourself.

A World Stopped

I will never forget 9/11/01.

We were in a meeting when the first plane hit. Our leader rolled in the TV, and we watched live as the second struck. Shock, tears, anger, denial - every person reacted differently. Some tried to keep working, furious when meetings were canceled. Others cried. Some joked to cope. I fell into the "joking for distraction" camp until the fear really hit.

There was so much confusion in the world about what was really happening. We were at a telecommunications company, which made it worse, as rumors spread that if the United States were under attack, we could be a target. Eventually, we were sent home, and we were all a bit dazed and confused. I remember the drive, the empty roads, the eerie silence, the flags already being lowered to half-mast.

That night, I rocked my baby to sleep and held her a little tighter, then tighter still. I remember wondering who could have done something so unimaginable and why. Did their mothers rock them to sleep when they were babies? Did they ever feel love like this?

I held my daughter close that night, and if I'm honest, I've held both my daughters close every day and night since.

That day taught me something I've carried into every leadership role since in a true crisis, no two reactions are the same. There're no right or wrong, only different ways of coping. A good leader recognizes that, stays calm, and leads with empathy.

Integrity Above All

And just when I thought the chaos was behind us, new challenges emerged. The program pressed on. We converted nearly 8,000 locations, a staggering number when I look back now. Along the way, whispers of corruption surfaced: people making shady bank runs and rumors of bribery. It didn't sit right with me, so we reported it. We did the right thing, even though it wasn't easy. Integrity has always been my compass, even when the path feels uphill.

Near the end of the project, I was offered the chance to join Cingular directly, a huge career milestone. But before that moment of celebration, pride and ego got the best of me. At a team dinner, a leader stood up and announced that *he* had "gotten us these jobs." I knew that wasn't true. Our hard work had earned those offers, not his influence. My blood boiled. Back in the office, I confronted him, slammed his door on the way out, and probably rattled the entire floor. I hit it so hard, I'm still shocked it stayed on the hinges.

It wasn't my best leadership moment, but it was real. I was tired, passionate, and fiercely protective of the truth, maybe a little too much so. But that day taught me something I still carry with me: leadership isn't about being perfect; it's about being principled. Thankfully, I still moved onward and upward, and with each step, I learned to pair my fire with grace.

Lessons Learned from Chapter Four

Believe in yourself. You are not your circumstances. Walk into the room anyway.

Listen to the client. Anticipate needs and deliver solutions before they ask.

Don't sweat the small stuff. Overreacting under stress can hurt your credibility and relationships.

In a crisis, remember this: every reaction is valid. Lead with empathy, especially when fear takes hold.

Protect your reputation. Say no to shortcuts or shady behavior. Integrity will sustain your career long after the titles fade.

5

Expansion with Flexibility

After the Cingular Wireless brand conversion, several of us were asked to remain employees. That was a huge compliment and proof that our work ethic and results stood out. For the first time since Wolf Camera, I felt like I wasn't just part of a project; I was part of something enduring.

It felt surreal to walk into AT&T's Atlanta headquarters, where just months earlier, I had been climbing around the unfinished floors of that same high-rise, nine months pregnant, trying to find the perfect signage placement. I still remember the battle over logo positioning, the debates with city planners, the visibility studies from the highway and MARTA, and the tension between brand visibility and executive window views. Back then, I was focused on signs. Now, I was focused on belonging in that office.

Instead of a construction site, I now entered a gleaming high-rise with marble floors and paneling, heading up to my cubicle on the 17th floor. The views were breathtaking. The first storm I watched from that window is etched in my memory - lightning flashing across the sky like a battle between good and evil. It was poetic in a way, the perfect metaphor for corporate life: bright moments of clarity followed by storms that could shake everything you'd built.

I didn't know it yet, but this new chapter would test not just my skills, but my flexibility and teach me that growth often comes disguised as change.

Building Something New

We still had plenty to do closing out the conversion, maintaining existing signage, and branding new locations. That included dealer and company-owned stores, drafting contracts, and working with procurement to secure suppliers.

Challenges came with the territory. My favorite? The case of the maggot-filled awning. A maintenance call revealed pigeons had nested inside the lights. When the issue was fixed, the pigeons died (or should I say fried) and that attracted maggots that fell onto customers walking into the store. Imagine explaining that one.

I loved that role and the director I worked for, but corporate restructuring hit, and soon I had a new leader. She had been with the company since the old "Ma Bell" days and knew everyone and their children. Networking was her superpower, and she pushed us to think bigger.

Local market leaders felt excluded from branding decisions, which created tension between corporate and retail. Our challenge? Fix it. With her backing, we created an internal website where local leaders could order signage, and we rewrote every supplier contract to standardize manufacturing standards and approvals.

The result was magic: better branding, smoother processes, and more collaboration between corporate and retail. It still stands as one of my biggest wins.

The Woman Who Led with Generosity

During this time, I met a woman who made an impression on me that changed my life and many others. She started a small business,

Service Select, just from recognizing companies needed help securing landlord approvals. Now it originally wasn't glamorous work, not high-paying, just honest hustle built to satisfy a need. I remember sitting across from her during one of those early meetings, watching her shuffle through paperwork while quietly admitting she wasn't sure how she would make payroll that month.

Most people would have quit right there. Not her.

Oh boy, did she keep going. Client after client. She would find a need in the industry and offer a service to fill it. She taught me so much: from gaining approval from the toughest landlords to getting meetings with the mayor to secure that permit. She worked harder than anyone I'd ever seen, but she also worked *differently*. She didn't just care about projects; she cared about people.

If we went out to a restaurant, she knew every server's name before we paid the check. She would ask about their families, their dreams, and sometimes their struggles, and she always remembered the details. It wasn't performative; it was who she was. She had a background in social services, and instead of leaving that gift behind, she folded it into her business.

Over the years, I watched her grow her company from three lovely ladies to a full-service signage company, one of the most respected in the industry. Not because she chased profit, but because she believed in paying it forward. She helped employees through personal crises, covered bills when people were too embarrassed to ask, and created a culture where generosity wasn't policy; it was identity.

Don't get it twisted, she certainly had her own battles. She had health issues and faced them with a smile. There were days she would have to show up with a cane or walker. She would get on that flight and be wherever she was supposed to be. I still don't know how she did it but I admire her for it. I have tried to mirror some of her silent strength and positivity throughout my own journey.

Watching her taught me that leadership isn't measured in titles or revenue or how perfectly your plans unfold. It's measured in how you make people feel and how much courage you inspire simply by being yourself.

She proved we could do it all: build families, build companies, build each other and do it without pretending to be anything but who we truly are.

Lessons in Facilities Management

Of course, corporate life loves a shake-up. Once the website was running smoothly, my role became redundant. But when one door closes, another opens, whether you're ready or not.

The director pulled me into Facilities Management, overseeing AT&T's Windward Campus, which included four buildings, 750,000 square feet, and 3,000 employees. It felt like running a small city. I wasn't ready. I loved branding and signage. I was known and respected in that arena, and I wasn't quite ready to move on. But I did like being employed, and I wasn't ready to leave AT&T.

Facilities management came with its own brand of crazy. It's one big lesson in human resources, and almost every day comes with a new and exciting story, like the family of beavers who set up shop near the creek, chewing trees to build their dam. The city required a certain number of trees on the property, and the beavers didn't care about compliance. We had animal activists on one side, property managers on the other, and me, in high heels, slipping through the mud with wildlife removal. I had a co-worker, who is now a dear friend, assigned to this specialty project because she's another one who will do whatever it takes to fix any situation. Thankfully, she had the beavers quietly relocated - or at least, that's what they told us, and we didn't ask any questions.

We also dealt with the IT department's explosive growth. Leadership packed employees into conference rooms until evacuation routes were blocked. To prove the danger, we called in the local fire marshal for a timed drill. We failed miserably, but that gave us the leverage we needed to enforce safety rules.

Facilities management wasn't glamorous, but it was formative. It taught me that leadership is about everything from safety and security to food service and fire codes. And sometimes, it's just about keeping 3,000 adults from acting like kids.

While I was learning to manage all that complexity at work, my personal life was unraveling in ways that tested me far more than any family of beavers ever could.

Strength Behind the Scenes

Facilities management wasn't the only new thing I was learning in that season. I was also learning to navigate the murky waters of divorce. Like many divorces, mine started somewhat amicable and quickly shifted into something far more complicated. When you have children, you want the process to be as clean and calm as possible - but mine was anything but.

When one party has unlimited access to litigation and the other does not, the result is a painfully uneven playing field. My divorce dragged on for over a year, and after spending more than $100,000 in attorney fees, I simply couldn't afford to keep going. The best thing I ever did, though I do **not** recommend this approach to anyone, was to walk into that courtroom alone and represent myself. I had no options left, and God must have known I had reached my limit because that day He sent an angel in the form of a female judge to preside over my case.

At one point, my ex-husband's attorney asked a question about a past hearing. I held up my stack of court papers and said, "I'm not sure which hearing you're referring to." The judge paused, looked at me, and asked how long this had been going on. I told her the truth. She turned to the attorney and warned him about abusive litigation, and just like that, the endless hearings stopped.

I didn't recover financially for a long time. In fact, I eventually filed for bankruptcy. But I never once regretted the decisions I made. The only thing that mattered to me was ensuring joint custody, the very thing we'd originally agreed to, and that's exactly where we landed. My attorney thought I was crazy for giving up so much, but none of that mattered. I knew I could rebuild. I had burned my life down before and started again, and I was prepared to do it one more time.

As hard as those days were, I refused to become bitter. I never spoke badly about the girls' father or the situation. That is important for anyone walking through divorce or conflict: your children deserve the freedom to love both parents without carrying out your battle. How you carry yourself in the most challenging moments reveals your character.

There were days I worked without sleep. Nights, I fed my family using the spare change from a piggy bank. I turned those meals into little adventures because I never wanted my daughters to feel the heaviness of the situation. I smiled even when I was breaking. I made them feel safe even when I felt like I couldn't take another breath.

This book isn't about divorce, and I won't air anyone's mistakes here; Lord knows we all make them. I share this only to say: **if you're going through something like this, you are not alone.** Focus on what truly matters. Don't worry about things or money; you can make more of that. Hold yourself together for the sake of the people who depend on you and show up to work like you've slept eight hours even when you haven't slept a wink.

Walking through that season made me stronger, but it also left me raw. Which is precisely why my next challenge felt so impossible: standing at a podium when I wasn't sure my voice would hold.

Fear at the Podium

During a safety kickoff, I experienced something I had never had before: a full-blown panic attack in front of 100 employees. My palms were sweating, my heart pounded so hard I could hear it in my ears, and my voice trembled like it belonged to someone else. For a split second, I thought about bolting from the room, but somehow, I powered through.

Later, someone teased me about the "broken microphone." There was nothing wrong with that microphone. It was just my terrified voice. I laughed it off in that moment, but inside, I was shaken. That day showed me what unchecked anxiety can do, how fear can sneak in, even when you're prepared, polished, and standing in front of your own team.

It was awful, but it also cracked open a door I didn't know I needed to walk through. That moment became the start of learning how to manage fear instead of letting it manage me, a lesson that would serve me far beyond that podium.

Back to Branding

After a few years in facilities and more wild stories than I could ever fit here, I returned to branding. AT&T needed another signage conversion, and this time hired CBRE to lead. It felt like coming home to something I loved. The project was massive and felt impossible, but to me, that just meant one thing: it was a challenge worth taking on.

We worked so closely together that you couldn't always tell who was CBRE and who was AT&T. I helped them build playbooks and processes, and they introduced me to a whole new world of acronyms. There were so many, I ended up creating a cheat sheet just to keep them straight.

Somewhere along the way, my desk became the unofficial therapy station. I taped up a sign that read *"Therapy 25 cents"* and spent countless lunches and late nights listening, laughing, and helping teammates untangle the day. I even bought a dream dictionary to help people interpret what their subconscious might be trying to tell them. Those conversations happened between marathon work sessions and late-night takeout runs, but they're the moments I remember most.

The project was a success, and afterward, I was invited to move to Dallas to continue branding for AT&T. But by then, life looked different. I was divorced, co-parenting my daughters, and deeply rooted in Georgia. Moving wasn't in the cards. Family came first. The decision wasn't easy, but I knew what mattered most. Success wouldn't mean anything if it came at the cost of not being present for my girls.

Not long after, CBRE approached me directly. I had been their client and built strong relationships with their team. They wanted me to bring my experience to their team. JLL was also an option, but CBRE stood out. They didn't have many women in project management leadership at the time, and I saw an opportunity to shake things up. I knew I could bring both my femininity and my unique flair to the table, and that sealed the deal.

I didn't know it then, but this next chapter would turn out to be one of the most defining of my career, the place where experience and grit would finally come together.

Lessons Learned from Chapter Five

You don't have to solve everything yourself. Great leaders empower their teams to create and trust in their own solutions.

Change never shows up when you're ready. Most growth starts the moment you're forced out of your comfort zone.

Cut down on the negative noise. When folks feel included, even the biggest complainers turn into your most valuable contributors.

Know when to call in help. Safety, integrity, and humility always come before pride.

Acknowledge fear, nerves, and anxiety. That discomfort usually means you're stretching into something new.

Prioritize family and health. You can have it all — just maybe not all at once.

6

The Climb

I did it. I transitioned from AT&T to CBRE, joining as a Senior Project Manager. My first assignment was a small AT&T conversion, so the move felt natural: the same client, the same work, and familiar faces.

But the longer I stayed, the more I realized CBRE was a whole new world. Professional. Polished. Competitive. A man's world, filled with MBAs, golf outings, and Ivy League pedigrees. I didn't have that background, but I didn't let it intimidate me. If anything, I let it drive me. I was determined to prove that experience, heart, and hustle could go toe-to-toe with any degree.

Remember, my original dream was to be a movie star. My "backup" dream? Dressing store windows or finding the perfect lipstick for women at a makeup counter. Corporate life wasn't exactly on my radar. But CBRE became my playground, my proving ground, and my chance to climb, stretch, and discover what confidence really looked like for me.

What I didn't know then was that this climb wouldn't just be about advancing my career. It would be about learning how to stand tall in rooms that weren't built for me.

Finding My Style

At first, I leaned into old AT&T relationships and my humor. I'd joke, "Y'all sure were nicer to me when I was the client." But soon, CBRE gave me opportunities I never imagined with mentorships, leadership programs, and training galore. Scary? Yes. Anxiety-inducing? Absolutely. But each challenge left me stronger and more confident in what I brought to the table.

There were moments early on when I felt utterly out of place. During one of my first client presentations, the room was packed with suits, spreadsheets, and Ivy League confidence. I walked in with my Southern accent, my humor, and my cheetah notebook. For a second, I thought about toning it down, speaking softer, blending in. But then I remembered something I'd learned long before: if you can't out-degree them, out-deliver them. So I cracked a joke, got the room laughing, and then delivered the cleanest rollout plan they'd seen. That day, I stopped apologizing for being different and started realizing it was my superpower.

Signage and brand conversions became my specialty, and that niche opened doors I never saw coming. It gave me access to executives, pitches, and clients, and taught me how to build high-functioning teams that could deliver on impossible timelines. I learned the art of pairing people with opposite skill sets and ideas: creatives with process junkies, veterans with rookies, dreamers with doers. Then I gave them clear playbooks, stood back, and let the magic happen.

I wasn't just leading programs, I was living in the trenches: wearing vendor badges at sign shops, learning lighting, and walking factory floors. Days, nights, weekends...whatever it took. I balanced toughness with fairness, grit with fun. I've been the first one to take a bullet, and the first one to dance on a table. That mix of authenticity and accountability built relationships that have lasted three decades and taught me that outstanding leadership isn't about power - it's about presence.

Family in the Mix

Career mattered, but my daughters came first. I wanted them to understand why I worked so hard - not just for survival, but to show them what women can accomplish, what they could accomplish.

I folded them into my work. My youngest prepped brand books in the backseat, while my oldest typed responses to emails from the front on my old Blackberry, dictation-style. They took their roles so seriously that when we drove past a store with a crooked banner, my daughter shouted, "Oh no, they didn't! Somebody's losing their job over this!"

Business trips often ended at hotels with pools, where we'd laugh at pageant moms rushing past us, panicking over perfection, while my girls swam freely and fearlessly. At home, they pitched me their Birthday and Christmas lists in PowerPoint, polished enough to rival Madison Avenue. Saying no was nearly impossible.

Bringing them into my world, instead of trying to keep work and home separate, became one of my greatest strengths as both a parent and a professional. It taught them the value of hard work and taught me that leadership doesn't stop at the office door. Years later, I shared that same advice with other working moms, especially during COVID, when the lines between home and career blurred completely.

The truth is, we're all juggling something. The goal isn't perfection, it's balance. It's learning how to make the mix not only bearable, but beautiful.

Building Leaders, Not Just Signs

At CBRE, I wasn't just the signage subject matter expert - I was building leaders. I talked people out of quitting, helped them find their superpowers, and when needed, delivered a well-timed kick in the pants. Nothing makes me prouder than seeing those careers soar. Watching someone find their confidence is like watching a light turn on and realizing you had a small part in clicking that switch.

After years of doing the "impossible," I finally said my next goal out loud: Director. For years, I had already been working at that level without the title or the pay, proving to myself that I could handle the responsibility. When the promotion finally came, it wasn't just a career win; it was a full-circle moment.

The person who promoted me was someone I remembered as a gas-soaked intern on his very first day. It reminded me, never underestimate the people around you. The intern you mentor today could be your CEO tomorrow. And when that happens, it's not a loss of power. It's proof that you led well.

Raising the Bar

I didn't stop at being promoted to Director. I began building the Brand Enhancement Services Team (BEST), bringing together experts to design new tools and models. We didn't just improve conversions - we reinvented how CBRE managed them.

We also reinvented how we trained suppliers. I'll never forget one kickoff: 75 suppliers in the room, my anxiety peaking, and then a foot cramp struck. My friend and colleague ordered me to take off my shoe, grabbed my foot, and squeezed the cramp out - just so we could start on time. Now that's loyalty. That's teamwork. And that's a friend!

From there, she and I raised the bar on everything we touched: events, presentations, training, and supplier summits. We obsessed over music, storyboards, menus, and décor, because every detail matters. Those weren't just meetings; they were experiences. They were relationship-building machines that made people feel valued and seen.

That's what authentic leadership is about: creating environments where people feel inspired to give their best - not because they have to, but because they *want* to. Looking back, those years at CBRE were about so much more than career growth. They were about proving that leadership doesn't have to fit into a box. You can be bright and stylish, bold and kind, demanding and deeply human. The climb wasn't just about rising in title - it was about growing into myself.

Lessons Learned from Chapter Six

Build a style that blends the personal and professional. Your kids don't need to be shut out of your work. Let them see the why, not just the what.

Volunteer for committees. Sometimes, the most minor roles open big doors and grow your network across business lines.

Build your team. Find loyal team members with all kinds of strengths you can pull together at a moment's notice. That's how you tackle the impossible.

Respect everyone. The intern you help today could be tomorrow's CEO. Treat them right.

Find your balance. Lead in the trenches, dance on tables, and know when to push and when to laugh.

7

Losing Authenticity

This is where my story starts to shift.

Up until now, I've preached: take all the free training you can get, learn from everyone, soak it all in. I still believe that one hundred percent. But here's the warning: don't ever train so much, or mold yourself so tight that you lose your authentic self. Stop the fear of not being good enough long before you stop being yourself.

That's what happened to me. Not overnight. Slowly. Subtly. Little by little. Until one day I realized I had become this overtrained machine - polished, almost great, but missing the personality, grit, and humor that made me, well, me.

The Climb Without Oxygen

Work and home were both going well, at least from outside. I had learned how to navigate the corporate landscape better than most, how to speak the language, anticipate politics, and play the game without getting caught. I attacked each rung of the ladder like it was set in stone, only to find that people kept moving steps, shifting priorities, or knocking me off balance altogether. Sometimes, they even used my climb as leverage for their own.

When people asked me what made me happy or what my hobbies were, I didn't have an answer. I'd smile and say: my kids, my family, my work. True, but not personal. Not about *me*. Somewhere along the way, I'd mixed up my identity with my output. My worth had quietly become tied to productivity, performance, and praise.

The higher I climbed, the thinner the air got. It felt like I was scaling a mountain - without oxygen, steady, determined, but gasping for something I couldn't quite name. I'd trained myself to push through fear, exhaustion, and even doubt, but not to stop and breathe.

And as I grew more successful, I started noticing how hard it was to take direction from others, especially men who hadn't come close to delivering what I had. I'd sit in meetings, listening to recycled ideas I'd presented weeks earlier, now rebranded as "strategic innovations." It burned, not because I needed credit, but because I wanted truth.

I was the rabbit running at full speed - chasing approval, chasing security, chasing something that always seemed just out of reach. And the faster I ran, the further I drifted from the real me.

The Pitch That Broke Me

It all came to a head during a massive pitch: the merger of SunTrust and BB&T to become Truist — one of the largest rebranding programs in history.

We prepared for months. That final week was hell. Basically, locked in rooms, over-coached by executives who didn't understand rebranding. Told how to hold our posture, tilt our heads, and ask fake questions. It wasn't a pitch anymore; it was theater.

Now, I grew up loving the stage, but this wasn't it. This wasn't joy or creativity; it was choreography. A real pitch should come from the heart, grounded in connection and truth. But fear had crept in. Fear of looking foolish. Fear of not being enough. Fear of losing everything I had worked for. So, I stayed quiet. I let them rewrite the story I was meant to tell.

The morning of the presentation, the sky opened up in Charlotte. Tornado sirens wailed through the city, a fitting omen if there ever was one. While our competitors bonded with the client in a stairwell, we were still practicing fake questions and forced smiles. I remember thinking, *we've already lost.* And we had.

When the real meeting began, the energy was all wrong. The client asked genuine, thoughtful questions, the kind I loved answering, and our executives deflected them like bullets, sticking to their scripts. I sat there in silence, knowing exactly what needed to be said, but the words stayed lodged in my throat.

When it was over, I walked out of that boardroom with a knot in my stomach. Not because we'd lost the pitch, but because I'd lost something much more important - my *voice.*

That night over wine, a friend and I debriefed. The food was good. The wine was better. But the truth stung: we weren't ourselves, it showed, and that would end up costing us.

The Silence That Haunts

Why didn't I speak up? Why didn't I stand for my team, my client, myself?

I had the answers. I had instincts. But I stayed quiet. And that's what haunted me.

It wasn't just impostor syndrome, though I didn't have that word for it back then. It wasn't just anxiety or overthinking. It wasn't just the little girl-in-me who still flinched at taking up too much space, who remembered every comment about her size or voice. It was all of it, knotted up inside me - like armor that was meant to protect, but all it did was make it harder to breathe.

The result? I let myself down. I let my team down. The worst part was knowing they had followed me because they trusted me. They believed in the version of me that was bold, fearless, and unapologetically real. But in that room, I wasn't her. I was a shell of her - a polished version who checked all the boxes but left her heart outside the door.

In the weeks that followed, I tried to shake it off, file it under "lessons learned," and move on. But that silence lingered. It followed me on walks, into meetings, into moments of success that should have felt like celebration but didn't. It made me question not just my decisions, but my direction.

That quiet reflection became something else entirely; it was my awakening. I realized the voice I'd silenced in that boardroom wasn't just my own. It was the voice of every woman who'd ever been told to tone it down, to wait her turn, to be grateful for that seat at the table. It was the voice of the girl who once danced fearlessly at the mall, who told stories with confidence and laughter, who believed she belonged anywhere she decided to stand.

The next time fear came calling, I promised myself I wouldn't let it mute me again. Because fear doesn't ever go away, you just learn to move through it.

Sometimes the worst part of our many life journeys is not the start, the challenging climb, or even the fall. It's sitting in the knowing that something isn't right, that justice wasn't done, or that you played a part in allowing something to happen to yourself or others. We need to listen to our instincts and speak up at times when it really matters.

From that point forward, I made myself a promise: when people put their trust in me to lead, I would not let them down again, not by losing my temper, not by losing control, and definitely not by losing my voice.

The Warning Signs

Looking back, I could see the warning signs were everywhere. I was running on fumes but telling everyone I was fine. My body was begging for rest, but I told myself it was just the hustle. My heart was anxious, but I pretended it was just my drive.

There were days I'd walk into the office with a smile so practiced, it felt like a mask. I'd sit in meetings, nodding along, while a quiet voice inside me whispered, *something's got to change.* But I didn't listen. I was too busy performing, leading, fixing, and proving...

That's the thing about losing authenticity: you don't lose it all at once. It slips away quietly: one compromise, one silence, one fake smile at a time. You start saying yes when you mean no, start turning down your own light just to keep others comfortable, and before long, you hardly recognize yourself.

Somewhere along the way, I lost my spark. That fire that once made me bold and full of laughter had faded to a flicker. I could still feel it, buried deep inside, but it wasn't lighting the way anymore. I missed her—the woman who could find humor in chaos, who believed in the impossible, who led with heart instead of fear.

I told myself it was just stress, just another season. But deep down, I knew better. I had become so focused on keeping everything running that I forgot to keep myself alive in the process. I was still moving, still producing, still climbing, but the joy was gone. The light was dimming.

And eventually, when you keep pushing through that kind of exhaustion, life has a way of making you stop and listen.

Lessons Learned from Chapter Seven

Stay true to yourself. No pitch, no training, and no title is worth losing your authenticity.

Know your worth. Don't shrink to fit or let fear convince you that your value needs validation.

Speak up. Instincts matter. Even if your voice shakes, let it be heard. Silence may feel safe in the moment, but it costs you pieces of yourself over time.

Protect your spark. The world will always ask for more of you, so don't give away the parts that make you uniquely shine.

8

The Fall

After the big pitch, we went back to work as if nothing had happened. It was almost business as usual. We were planning for the conversion as if we had won, lining up teams, building playbooks, mapping out technology platforms, and scheduling kickoff calls that would never come. On the outside, I did what I was supposed to do: smile, nod, and keep everyone moving forward. On the inside, my gut was screaming the truth. We weren't going to win this one.

I remember the morning the news hit. I was working from home that day, but I could feel the unusual tension in the air. I got fewer emails than usual; the ones I received were short and appeared clipped. Then the message came through. It was simple, cold, and official: We lost the bid. Thanks to those who participated. We will have a debriefing meeting in the near future.

I just sat there staring at my screen, waiting for it to sink in. All the months of planning, the sleepless nights, the over rehearsed pitch. All that sacrifice, gone in one email.

For a long time, I didn't move. The sun was coming through my office window and felt warm on my skin. Then came the sting behind my eyes, the tightness in my chest, and the wave of anger that always comes before grief.

I wasn't just mad about losing the pitch. I was heartbroken because this was supposed to be *the one*. The Truist rebrand was the kind of project that could have finally funded BEST, the Brand Enhancement Services Team I'd spent over a decade building - sometimes with nothing more than a big dream and a handful of loyal believers. We had worked so hard to prove ourselves, to show that a small team with big ideas could move mountains. And for a moment, it looked like we might actually do it.

But just like that, the dream slipped away. The carrot I'd been chasing for years yanked out of reach again, and I was too tired to chase it anymore.

Still, I did what I always did. I pulled myself together, straightened my blazer, and got back to work. Because that's what women like me are taught to do: show up, smile through it, and keep moving. But something inside me shifted that day.

It wasn't just the loss of a contract. It was the loss of blind faith, the belief that hard work and loyalty would always pay off, that doing the right thing guaranteed the right outcome.

I didn't know it then, but that would be the last time I let someone else control the finish line. The last time I poured everything I had into something that wasn't aligned with my truth.

I just didn't know the world was about to test that lesson even further. Because 2020 had only just begun, and it was bringing a storm none of us could have prepared for.

A Pandemic Shakes the World

Right about then, the world got hit with a global pandemic - first called the coronavirus, now known as COVID-19.

At first, it didn't seem real. It sounded more like something from a movie. Then the emails started. Meetings canceled. Flights grounded. Rumors about offices closing. The entire world was shifting, and for once, no one had a playbook.

Right before the first lockdown, I was asked to give the "safety moment" on a global call. It sounds small, but at the time, it felt like the biggest stage of my life. The speakers were all high-level executives, polished, confident, seasoned voices that carried authority even through a screen. I was terrified. My hands shook so hard I could barely keep my notes still. I even faked a sore throat in one of the rehearsals just so no one would notice how shaky my voice was.

But this was different. People's lives were literally at stake. This wasn't about branding, signage, or performance metrics. This was about human beings. They were scared, uncertain, and looking for direction. So, I studied science, listened to global reports, and reminded myself: *this isn't about me.* This is about empathy, compassion, and care.

The day of the call, I skipped my coffee, did my power poses in the mirror, whispered a prayer, and hit "Join Meeting." My voice trembled at first, but I kept going. I talked about washing hands, about staying calm, about leading with grace instead of panic. It wasn't perfect, but it was honest - and in that moment, honesty felt like exactly what people needed most.

Then the world shut down. Offices closed. Airports went quiet. My daughters came home from college, their classes suddenly on Zoom, and we all found ourselves back under one roof, trying to make the best of something terrifying.

The first few days were a blur of fear and news updates. But slowly, life found a strange new rhythm. We cooked dinners together, swam in the pool, played Guitar Hero, and laughed more than I thought we would. We were grateful just to be together. For a little while, the world stopped spinning so fast, and I realized how much I had missed the simple act of slowing down.

Outside, the streets were empty. But inside our house, there was laughter, music, and the smell of something baking almost every day. We were building memories in the middle of a storm. It was the good part of an awful situation.

Meanwhile, I found myself coaching working mothers who were barely holding it together. Calls would come in from colleagues whispering through bathroom doors while their toddlers hollered in the background. I told them what I knew from years of balancing children and work: set them up with a desk, give them tasks, offer grace to them and to yourself, and remember nobody's perfect.

I could see the exhaustion in their eyes even through the screen, and I recognized it. It was the same look I'd seen in my own reflection more times than I could count. The look of someone trying to hold everything together, afraid to let one thing slip for fear the whole world might fall apart.

The truth was, I didn't have all the answers. None of us did. But sometimes leadership isn't about knowing everything, it's about showing up anyway. And deep down, I could feel it again, that quiet whisper that always comes before a major life shift.

The storm was far from over.

The Layoff

Then came the call.

It came late in the evening, at the end of an extremely long, heavy day. I had just turned off work for the day and headed to the basement for a bit of TV watching with the family. I saw a familiar number, so I answered,

"Hi, Darlia, do you have a minute?"

There was a pause, then: "I don't know how to tell you this."

That tone was soft, rehearsed, and careful, and I knew it before they said another word. My stomach dropped. I braced myself and said, "You don't have to, I already know." He apologized over and over again, and I let him know it was ok, and I understood. The truth is, none of us really understands what happens when that happens. I just didn't want him to feel bad, because I know how hard it is to make those calls.

After that, I stopped hearing anything. The rest was a blur of corporate jargon and HR comforting clichés. Words like *"realignment "*and *"budget impacts"* floated around while my brain screamed, *"This can't be happening during a global pandemic".*

When the call ended, I just sat there, staring at a dark TV screen as I had turned it off and the room had emptied.

A high-level executive later told me it should not have happened. I wasn't "supposed" to be on that list. Maybe a clerical error, maybe politics. But none of that mattered in the moment. The truth was simple: I got the call with HR paperwork.

I felt angry, hollow, and betrayed all at once. After building programs that had generated enough revenue to fund a small city, this was my thank-you? I had given everything - my time, energy, late nights, early mornings, the best years of my life - and suddenly, it was over.

But I didn't have the luxury of falling apart. As the sole provider for my family, I didn't have time to sulk or spiral. I needed to land on my feet.

So, I took a deep breath, opened my laptop, and updated my LinkedIn with three simple words: Open to Work.

Within hours, my phone started lighting up. Messages, calls, and emails poured in with people I hadn't heard from in years reaching out with encouragement, job leads, and words that went straight to my heart. "You're too good to stay down for long." "We'd be lucky to have you." "I still remember what you taught me."

That's when it hit me: my real value wasn't in a title or a salary. It wasn't tied to an email signature or a corner office. My worth was in people, in the relationships I'd built, the teams I'd grown, the careers I'd helped shape, and the companies I'd helped develop. That realization was equal parts humbling and healing.

I cried real, messy tears, the kind that come when gratitude meets exhaustion. Then I got up, wiped my face, and got to work answering every message, considering every offer, and listening to every piece of advice. For the first time in weeks, I felt something that had been missing: hope.

It felt like confirmation that I was exactly where I needed to be on the edge of something new.

And then someone from CBRE called.

A new role had opened on the Chase account. It sounded like stability, like safety, like a lifeline. But the moment I hung up, my gut clenched. Red flags everywhere.

Still, fear is a powerful persuader. The weight of being the only paycheck, the only safety net, pressed heavily on my chest. I told myself it was temporary, that I'd figure it out later, that it was the practical thing to do.

So, I said yes. I stayed.

And I would learn soon enough what ignoring that little voice inside you can cost.

The Red Flags I Ignored

The new director told me flat-out, "I don't know why you're here. We don't need you."

Ouch, that stung in a way that left a mark. Not because I didn't believe in my own value, but because I did, and I knew exactly what I brought to the table. Still, I smiled politely, nodded, and told myself to push through. I'd weathered more brutal storms. But deep down, my gut whispered the truth I didn't want to hear, *you shouldn't be here.*

I tried to drown that voice by working hard, convincing myself that things would get better. After all, the clients were great, a fantastic group of energized women who reminded me why I loved branding in the first place. We collaborated and explored new ways to improve. They made the work worthwhile. But when the laptop closed at night, the unease crept back in. I'd traded inspiration for obligation, traded peace for predictability.

During those few "Open to Work" days, I had met another company, a pure branding company, not a real estate firm that happened to handle branding on the side. Their leaders inspired me. Their culture felt alive, creative, and authentic. In every conversation, I felt a spark that had been missing for a while. I saw myself in their mission. I belonged there.

I even accepted their offer.

And then fear showed up.

Fear of the unknown. Fear of losing financial security. Fear that I might not live up to the expectations I'd set for myself, or worse, that I would, and it still wouldn't be enough. So, I called and declined. Told myself I needed "stability." Told myself I was being "responsible by staying." The truth? I was scared.

But the dream didn't go away. It followed me through the long nights, the forced smiles, the polite corporate calls that felt hollow. I couldn't stop thinking about it. I'd float around my swimming pool for hours, staring up at the sky, asking myself the same question: *If not now, when?*

Finally, one morning, I listened to that quiet inner voice that had been patiently waiting for its turn. I reached back out. The job was still there, almost as if it had been waiting for me to finally choose myself.

So, I took it. Even with the pay cut. Even with the risk. Because for the first time in a long time, I was ready to choose joy over judgment, alignment over anxiety, and authenticity over fear.

It wasn't just a new job. It was a new beginning.

For the first time in years, I felt peace instead of pressure, joy instead of proving. I had spent so long climbing ladders that leaned against somebody else's wall. This time, I was building my own.

The fall had finally taught me how to rise.

It was time to stop chasing carrots dangled by someone else and finally follow the leader inside me.

Lessons Learned from Chapter Eight

Trust your gut. If the flags are red, don't turn a blind eye.

Your value isn't your title. It's in your impact, your relationships, and the people you lift along the way.

Don't let fear dictate your future. Comfort zones are cozy, but you can't grow if you never stretch beyond them.

Crisis brings clarity. Even in the hardest seasons, laughter, family, and the little joys that matter most.

Choose what lines up with your heart, not just what wins approval. Sometimes the right path might pay less, but it'll bring you more purpose.

9

The Authentic Rise

One of the most exciting parts about the company I was about to join, I haven't even shared with you yet. Sit down and listen to this one.

This company was our competitor during the Truist pitch. Yes, the one that bonded with the client in the stairwell during the tornado drill, while all we heard was the tornado siren echoing in our ears. The one that followed the rules and gave the client exactly what they asked for. And now, I was about to join them.

Because of the pandemic, they were a little slow off the starting block, but that timing worked in my favor. It let me step into the kind of program I was born to run - the biggest, the fastest, the one most people would say was impossible. Move over, world, I was finally here.

But let me pause for a reality check. You know what they say: "Be careful what you wish for." That line exists for a reason. I thought there was no challenge that was too big for me - after all, 8,000 site conversions didn't even make me blink anymore. But doing that during a global pandemic, with supply chain chaos, and labor shortages? That's a whole different story. Welcome to the new frontier. Let's get it.

I started my new role as Vice President of PMO at Principle Global the day after my birthday. At first, it was a secret. I couldn't post it on

LinkedIn yet, and I wanted to settle in quietly before every supplier I had ever known started calling me.

That first week, I drove from Atlanta to Knoxville for training. The best part? The drive took me right through Cleveland, Tennessee. I got to spend Sunday nights at my parents' house and head to Knoxville early Monday morning. At fifty years old, it felt funny sleeping in my old room again. For a moment, I was a teenager. Honestly, I think my parents loved it just as much as I did.

The first week on the job was awkward in ways only 2020 could deliver. People were back in the office, but each person had their own rules. Some wore masks, some didn't. Some shook hands, others looked offended if you offered. Chairs were left empty for social distancing, the office manager walked around constantly spraying disinfectants, and half the training was in person while the other half was by phone. I leaned toward the cautious side but adjusted quickly. Looking back, it doesn't matter who was right or wrong. At the time, though, every little choice felt like a battle.

Even with the awkward start, the employees welcomed me. I was learning their processes, figuring out how they worked, and settling in. With another leader handling the overall program, my focus was on the retail side of the business. Yes, it was the largest and most visible, and yes, it carried the most pressure. But it was also squarely in my wheelhouse. I thought this would be a slam dunk.

I had no idea this new chapter would test me in ways I had never been tested before.

This time, I wasn't climbing for titles or chasing carrots. I was climbing to prove something entirely different: that success without authenticity isn't really success at all.

Finding My Voice Again

Something changed the moment I joined Principle. Maybe it was the creative energy, or perhaps it was just being around those familiar

East Tennessee accents. I spoke that language fluently, even though I'd spent my whole career trying to get rid of it.

I remember my uncle once told me, "If you don't get rid of that accent, people will assume you're dumb." I took that to heart. I never entirely lost my Southern drawl, but I was overcompensated with hard work and perfection. I used to record myself for hours, practicing how to smooth out that Tennessee twang. But now, for the first time, I didn't have to.

It didn't matter how I said the words, just that I said them. After a week in the Knoxville office, I called home, and my husband barely recognized my voice. The accent had come back full force, thick as honey.

Whatever it was, I started to feel more like *me* again - the version of me who laughed easily, who led with both intuition and grit, who didn't have to edit every word before speaking it out loud. Granted, that can be both good and bad, but I found my rhythm again.

I started bringing new ideas to the table, not just the polished ones but the half-baked ones that sparked better conversations. And little by little, I felt the spark returning, the fire that used to fuel me. It wasn't about proving anymore; it was about contributing.

For the first time in a long time, I wasn't just surviving leadership. I was enjoying it.

Calm Before the Storm

Those first few months at Principle felt like breathing again after holding my breath for years. I had my spark back, my confidence, and my voice, twang and all. Work was busy, but fulfilling, the kind that kept me up at night for the right reasons. My girls were thriving, life felt steady, and for once, I wasn't chasing anything.

It's funny how peace can trick you into thinking the climb is over. What I didn't know then was that this calm wasn't an ending; it was the deep inhale before the biggest test of my leadership life.

Lessons Learned from Chapter Nine

Timing matters. What feels like a setback today might just be setting you up for the perfect opportunity tomorrow.

Big things don't scare you - until they do. Even the most seasoned leaders get tested when the rules (and the world) change overnight.

Authentic rises start with being honest with yourself. Winning matters, but how you show up matters just as much.

Be flexible when you walk into something new. Sometimes the first test isn't the work; it's learning to fit into the culture.

Stay grounded. Whether in a high-rise office or your childhood bedroom, remembering where you came from will steady you for where you're headed.

Find your voice (again). Don't let the world polish the fire out of you. Speak with conviction, with your accent, with passion - every bit of it.

10

The Test of Authentic Leadership

Stepping Into the Storm

When I joined Principle, I figured I was stepping back in order to eventually step up. I had no idea just how fast or how big this opportunity turned out to be.

I was brought over to lead the retail portion of the program. It was high visibility, high pressure, and right in my wheelhouse. Then, almost overnight, everything changed. The lady who hired me left. Another VP left. And suddenly, I wasn't leading one part; I was leading all of it—fourteen lines of business, including sports, entertainment, and marketing.

It was the kind of challenge that'd make most people run for cover, but by then, I'd learned: when the world tilts, you straighten your spine. Leadership isn't about waiting for calm skies; it's about learning how to steer through the storm.

So, I did what I always do: I started building. Not just a team, but the *right* team. The kind of people who don't flinch under pressure, who laugh in chaos, and who can turn a wall of problems into a plan before breakfast. Some of the top talents I'd help develop at CBRE joined me. These were the same people I had once felt I'd let down during the Truist pitch. The fact that they believed in me enough to follow me to a new company was both humbling and powerful.

I wasn't just leading a team; I was rebuilding trust both in them and in myself.

Leading Through the Unthinkable

Then came the real test: pulling off one of the largest and most complex programs I'd ever seen, right smack dab in the middle of a global pandemic.

Labor shortages. Supply chain failures. Raw material shortages that would have brought any other program to a halt. We had to become problem solvers at a level that felt almost military.

The volume of messages coming in would have shocked Ma Bell. I had thousands of emails, texts, and phone calls per day. I knew each one brought a new problem that needed to be solved at light speed. My anxiety hit record highs and nearly shut me down, but the team was there - people who had left careers to follow me. So I took deep breaths, put on my lipstick, and kept moving forward.

We became a think tank for innovation. Every obstacle forced us to get creative. At one point, our program portal had more than 100,000 contacts. The client had 377 brand changes to document, and each one had to be communicated, tracked, and trained across every line of business. With so many vendors, manufacturers, and crews involved, every adjustment felt like redirecting a small city in real time.

We came up with fourteen different countermeasures for materials. A regular program might have one or two, but we needed a backup for every possible failure. If one paint color was delayed, we had another ready and waiting. If the metal finish couldn't ship, we found a local fabricator. We even found painters for our suppliers when COVID wiped out whole shop teams. Every day was a master class in crisis management.

At one point, we ran scenario tests like a military exercise, what to do if crews were quarantined, if shipping was disrupted, or even if communications went completely down. We had backup plans for our backup plans. And during the big unveil, we brought in out-of-state crews ready to deploy at a moment's notice.

We also held supplier roundtables where we challenged each other to find "impossible" solutions. Some days, morale was low and exhaustion high, but quitting was never an option. We worked long hours under relentless pressure, and somehow, laughter and tears shared through screens became our therapy. When you can cry, curse, and laugh in the same call and still hang up saying, "We've got this," that's when leadership becomes real.

We didn't sleep much, and the stress was relentless, but we did it. It wasn't a perfect program, but it was one of the proudest accomplishments of my career. To this day, suppliers and employees still reach out to thank me for not letting them quit when things got hard.

When the dust settled, I remember sitting outside one night, looking up at the sky - tired, humbled, and changed. I finally understood that leadership isn't about control. It's about courage, consistency, and the quiet strength to keep showing up when everyone else wants to give up. That kind of success doesn't fade. It becomes part of your leadership DNA.

Redefining Success

When the big weekend unveil was over, I remember standing in the break room with the team, champagne in hand. We clinked glasses, smiled for pictures, and tried to take it in. But the celebration only lasted a few moments. There was still too much left to do to close the program.

That night, I went back to my hotel, turned off the lights, and lay in bed completely spent. My body ached, my mind raced, and tears rolled down my cheeks. I wasn't sure if it was relief, pure exhaustion, or just the weight of realizing how much work was still ahead. Maybe it was all of it.

When the program finally wrapped, exhaustion hit us all like a wave. Many team members moved on to new roles or even new companies, and I understood why. That project had tested every part of who we were mentally, physically, and emotionally.

But for me, it clarified something bigger. I finally understood *why* I was at Principle. It wasn't just about flawless execution or checking off milestones on a spreadsheet. It was about transforming culture by building something rooted in authenticity, positivity, and integrity.

That experience didn't just prove what I could lead through. It proved who I could be while leading. And that, to me, was the real win.

The Reflection

When the noise finally quieted, it took almost another year. I realized leadership isn't measured in awards, promotions, or perfect programs. It's measured in the people who rise beside you, the ones who discover their own strength because you believe in them.

Sometimes, that belief propels them in directions you didn't expect. They grow, they move on, and that can break and fill your heart at the same time. You wonder if you could have done something different to change the way they see their future. But I've learned you can't. We're all here to find our own paths, and each one looks a little different.

I used to think success meant reaching the top of the mountain, but now I know it's about who you bring with you, how you lift them along the way, and whether you can look in the mirror at the end of it all and still recognize the person staring back.

That's what authentic leadership really is: the courage to lead without losing yourself.

As I started reflecting on the kind of leader I wanted to be moving forward, I realized I'd learned to lead through chaos, uncertainty, and exhaustion - but now, I wanted to lead with more authenticity and heart.

The funny thing is, just when I thought I had this whole "authentic leadership" thing figured out, the South went and taught me one more lesson.

Enter what I call *"Knoxville Nice."*

Knoxville Nice

There's something I had to relearn when working back in the South. Now, don't get me wrong, Atlanta is still the South, honey, right smack dab in the middle of it. But the larger corporate environments I'd been in for years didn't exactly allow much talk about religion, politics, or pillow talk. (And no, that's not allowed in most professional environments - I just threw it in there to keep you awake.)

When I started spending more time in Knoxville, I was reintroduced to a language I'd nearly forgotten, the one I call *"fake nice"* or *"Southern nice."* It's that sweet Southern drawl saying, *"Bless your heart"* or *"I'll be praying for you,"* and sometimes those words are sincere. But other times, they're sugar coating for frustration, judgment, or just plain avoidance.

See, in the South, we've mastered the art of looking someone straight in the eye, smiling, and hiding exactly what we think behind a casserole dish and a compliment - but in business, that can be dangerous.

I've seen "Knoxville Nice" stop honest feedback dead in its tracks. Teams get stuck because no one wants to say what really needs to be said. They stay polite but unproductive, cordial but disconnected. I've watched people praise others in public and undermine them in private, all in the name of *being nice.*

Now, I'm not saying we need to swap niceness with cruelty. I'm saying leadership deserves and demands truth. You can deliver it with care, compassion, and even a biscuit, but you've got to speak it, even if it's uncomfortable.

Authentic leadership means having hard conversations before problems fester. It means coaching people honestly, holding them accountable, and giving feedback that helps them grow, not just to survive. It means showing your team that kindness without honesty isn't kindness at all.

Lessons Learned from Chapter Ten

Leadership isn't about avoiding chaos; it's about staying grounded in the middle of it.

The best leaders don't demand trust; they earn it, one decision and one honest moment at a time.

There's always a solution, even when it feels like the world is falling apart. You just have to be brave enough to look for it.

Motivation matters. When people believe in you, they'll follow you anywhere. And when you believe in them, they'll rise even higher.

Authentic leadership isn't about holding on. It's about lifting others up and trusting you've done enough for them to fly on their own. That's what we want, not just for our employees, but for our children too.

11

The Chapter I Never Saw Coming

The Calm Before the Curveball

Life had finally found its rhythm. Work was busy but fun again, a far cry from the chaos of one of the most significant brand mergers in history. For the first time in years, I could breathe. I wasn't running on fumes or chasing deadlines that stole my weekends.

I had space to look up and really *see* my daughters. One was graduating from college, the other was getting ready to study at Oxford. Watching them step into their own adventures filled me with a mix of pride and awe. They had grown into strong, curious, independent women, and seeing that reminded me just how far we'd all come together.

So, the three of us took a European vacation. The trip was my gift to us, a long-overdue exhale. We strolled through the streets of London, admired the art in Paris, and laughed until we cried. The moment we arrived in Scotland, people started asking *us* for directions. I'm sure it was a combination of our red and auburn hair, our Scottish roots, and the confidence of three women who finally looked like they belonged right where they were.

It was the kind of trip that sticks to your soul. For me, it was especially meaningful because the first time I ever traveled outside the country, I was doing it with my daughters by my side.

When we returned, life still felt beautifully balanced. I was happy at work, content at home, and for once, had the bandwidth to focus on myself.

Years of long hours and stress had taken their toll, and my weight had climbed to a personal high. I was tired not just physically, but mentally, from carrying it all. After years of trying every diet and exercise plan under the sun, I decided to take a new approach. I met with a surgeon, scheduled the procedure, and went forward with a gastric sleeve.

The surgery itself went smoothly, but the recovery wasn't easy. I had to relearn what my body needed and when to listen to it. My husband was there for every appointment, every protein shake, every tough day. His quiet presence was a gift, especially when I didn't yet have the strength to celebrate small wins. Now hear me out on this one, he didn't care if I had the surgery or not. He has loved me at every size and found me sexy even when the scale hit its all-time high.

Now, this isn't a book about weight loss, though it's undoubtedly been a thread woven through my story. I don't want the focus to be on the number on the scale, but on what it represents: another chapter of courage. Weight loss surgery isn't an easy fix; it's a tool that demands discipline, patience, and a whole lot of hydration.

It took about 2 years to lose 100 pounds. I felt lighter, stronger, and freer than I had in years. For the first time in a long time, I was truly enjoying the calm.

But just when I thought I'd found peace, life had other plans.

The calm I'd worked so hard for was about to be replaced by something entirely new - and a whole lot hotter than I ever imagined.

Hot flashes!

The Hot Flash Chronicles

Let me just start by saying how completely naïve I was on this topic. That's partly because it's not something proper Southern women discuss, and partly because I absolutely, one hundred fifty percent, thought it didn't apply to me.

I thought I had skated through menopause. I'd smile politely when other women talked about it, maybe even toss in an "oh my" or a "bless your heart," but deep down, I was thinking, *I don't know what the big deal is.* A few mood swings, a few stray facial hairs, nothing I couldn't handle.

Then, out of nowhere, like a thief in the night, those hot flashes took over my life.

When they start, they don't care about your calendar, your career, or your composure. The bigger the meeting, the hotter the flash. If I were presenting on camera, my face would flush bright red, and sweat would roll down my back like I'd just finished a Slimnastics class, or a Jane Fonda workout video. No one could tell if I was having a panic attack or just "going through the change," as my grandmothers used to say.

One time, I was riding in the back seat of my dad's truck and suddenly felt heat radiating from behind me. "Who turned on the heated seat?" I asked. My parents started laughing. "Honey, the truck doesn't *have* heated back seats." That was the moment I realized the heat was all me.

But here's the thing: I was not about to go through life with my days and nights ruined by this nonsense. I started polling friends like I was running a medical focus group. One coworker told me, "You just have to deal with it." She offered natural remedies, black cohosh, soy, and meditation, but ended with a warning about hormone replacement therapy. "You know that can cause breast cancer," she said gently. She was a breast cancer survivor.

As she kept talking, I heard only one thing: *Get to a gynecologist immediately and get hormone replacement therapy, because it can stop these devilish hot flashes.*

You know me, I'm a woman of action. I went to the doctor so fast I didn't pass Go, and I sure didn't collect two hundred dollars. I showed up with my mammogram records in hand like I was checking into the ER for a miracle cure. They drew some blood, nodded knowingly, and confirmed what I already suspected: full-blown menopause.

They handed over the prescription, and let me tell you, it was like magic sunshine in pill form. Within a couple of months, I was cool, calm, mostly collected, and maybe a little too confident. I felt like I was in my twenties again. You name it, I could do it, including running with scissors.

Then came the holidays. I had my routine mammogram, the kind I'd done for years without a second thought. A few days later, I got the dreaded phone call.

"Hi, Ms. Clark. Can you come back in for a more detailed mammogram?"

"Sure," I said casually. "Let's get the holidays over, and I'll come in toward the new year."

We'd just got a new puppy for Christmas, and I wasn't about to interrupt our holiday fun for what was probably nothing. But then she said, "Ma'am, I need you to come in the day before Christmas Eve. This is important; it can't wait."

My heart sank. I hesitantly made the appointment, telling myself it was probably just a better image or a shadow. Weight loss could even be a factor. But at the appointment, their tone shifted. They were polite but vague, never a good sign, and told me I needed to see a specialist right away for a biopsy.

Now it felt real. And I was starting to get scared.

Still, I refused to take the focus away from the holidays. I smiled through family dinners, wrapped presents, and watched Christmas movies as if nothing was wrong. On the outside, everything was merry and bright. On the inside, fear was whispering, *what if this is serious?*

After Christmas, I went to the specialist. They did another mammogram and still didn't like what they saw. The doctor handed me the images and scheduled a biopsy.

I took that film home and studied it like my life depended on it. I wasn't exactly sure what I was looking for, but that didn't stop me from turning into Dr. Google. I zoomed in on every shadow, every line, comparing it to medical diagrams like I was starring in my own episode of *Grey's Anatomy*.

Deep down, I already knew something was different this time.

Diagnosis and Shock

The day of the biopsy came, and my husband drove me. I wasn't prepared for how involved it would be. I remember lying face down on a table with my breast through a hole. Then the table shifted, and the machine clicked and removed a section. The sound was sharp and metallic, and to this day, I still hear that click when the room is too quiet.

After the biopsy, it was right back to work. Those few days waiting for results felt like an eternity. I tried to maintain a strong composure so as not to alarm anyone.

I was working in my home office one afternoon on a Zoom call when I saw my doctor's number pop up. I excused myself, took a deep breath, and answered, trying to steady my hands.

I can't remember everything she said, but I remember these words: "You have two kinds of cancer, both invasive and noninvasive ductal carcinoma."

She told me to come in so we could start to make a plan.

After that, I don't remember much. The room felt like it was closing in, and my hearing went fuzzy. I thanked her for calling, hung up, and slowly walked upstairs to tell my husband.

He was folding laundry. He put down the clothes, listened, and held me, telling me everything would be alright and that he'd be with me every step of the way. He was so brave at that moment. But as I left the room, I heard him sobbing. I know I wasn't supposed to listen to that, and I never really brought it up. He is my silent strength and always knows how to help me before I even realize I need it. I didn't go back in that room that day partly out of respect for his private moment, and partly because I needed to keep it together so I could be there for him.

Then it was time for me to tell the rest of the family. I focused on the positives: I hadn't missed a mammogram, we caught it early, and breast cancer treatments had come a long way.

When I met with the doctor, I learned that not all breast cancer comes in lumps. Mine looked more like spiderwebs on the ultrasound. Because it was spreading so fast, it was classified as grade three, and we needed to be aggressive.

I chose a double mastectomy. I tried to keep it light, joking that at least I'd get a slight tummy tuck out of the deal. Before surgery, I asked friends and colleagues to promise they'd do one fun thing every day while I recovered. That was my way of showing strength and a little positivity in the middle of one of the hardest chapters of my life.

The Fight

The surgery was tough, and the recovery was tougher.

From the moment I woke up, my life changed forever. The nurses at Northside Hospital were like angels. One, named Nana, had such confidence that we convinced my husband to go home and rest. I knew I'd rely on him completely when I got home, so he needed sleep.

The day after surgery, I fainted on my way to the restroom. My daughter was visiting, and when my blood pressure bottomed out, she passed out on the other side of the room. I was scared but tried to stay calm for her. I kept telling the nurses I could feel my toes, even though

I wasn't sure I could. They stabilized me, but I never did get to remove my fall-risk bracelet.

That night, Nana came back. She told me she'd been praying she'd get assigned to me again. I don't know how she did it, but she had a way of making me and others feel safe.

When I was finally released, my husband drove me home, careful as could be, trying to make the ride as smooth as butter. At home, he watched over me, emptied my drains when I couldn't. Those drains were awful. When I caught a glimpse of them in the mirror, I felt like a monster, or a spider, with tubes coming out of my body. I wouldn't change my decision, but I do wish someone had prepared me for that part.

The hardest lesson was realizing that the best path forward changes constantly in cancer recovery. That's tough for someone who built a career on control, structure, and precision. I could lead teams and navigate programs that others said couldn't be done, but I couldn't control this.

So, I had to let go and let God. It was all in the hands of the professionals, and thankfully, I had some of the best.

All I could control was my attitude, my willingness to follow orders, and my commitment to stay positive.

I had always been the leader, the fixer, the one others leaned on. But this time, I had to learn, to lean, and to let others carry me. That kind of surrender felt foreign at first, but it taught me a deeper sort of humility and the strength to receive.

At first, I felt embarrassed about not being able to get up or even use the bathroom by myself. I hated to bother others for help. But through that humility, I learned something important: we all need help at certain times in our lives. Allowing others to care for us isn't weakness; it's grace in motion.

The battle didn't end with the mastectomy. I later had a hysterectomy and started with five years of medications that block hormones completely. You know what that means. Yes, we are right back to where this all started — those damn hot flashes!

Cancer took parts of me I can never replace, but it also gave me clarity I didn't know I needed. It stripped away every illusion of control, leaving me with gratitude, faith, and a renewed sense of purpose.

Although this was a chapter I didn't see coming, it changed how I live, lead, and love. I still mourn the person I used to be, but I rejoice in the woman I am becoming. I don't fully know her yet, but she's developing every day.

Lessons Learned from Chapter Eleven

You can't control everything. Sometimes, authentic leadership means surrender, trusting others, trusting God, and trusting the process.

Protect your health before your hustle. Careers are temporary, but your body carries you through your entire life's journey.

Clarity comes in crisis. Cancer strips away all the distractions and shows you who and what truly matters.

There is strength in vulnerability. Letting others help doesn't make you weaker; it just makes you human.

Grace in recovery is its own kind of power. Healing takes time, patience, and faith in yourself and those around you.

Redefine success. It's not about climbing ladders anymore. It's about living fully and loving deeply no matter the scars you carry - internal or external - they've made you who you are.

12

What's Next

Life after cancer, "I survived. Now what?"

When I had my first survivor appointment with the oncologist, I thought life would go back to normal. It didn't. It never does. You can't go back; you can only rebuild.

I remember that appointment clearly. Everyone around me was excited, but inside, I wasn't. I smiled, said all the right "yay" words, and called everyone who wanted to hear the good news. But I wasn't celebrating. I was still scared. Still wondering, *what's next?*

It didn't feel like I'd crossed a finish line; it felt more like I'd been dropped at the starting line of a brand-new race. The track looked unfamiliar; there were turns I couldn't predict, fear waiting around every corner, new tests, new doctors, and the quiet question of when or if cancer might try to catch me again. Death had chased me before and missed, but now it felt like it was still somewhere out there on the course.

None of us ever really knows where the finish line is, nor should we dwell on it. But once you've seen that shadow up close, you never forget it's there.

I was still on life-saving medications, still having hot flashes and mood swings, and there wasn't much femininity left in my once overly feminine body. I mean, it still looked feminine, but it was hard to feel that way without hormones and all the amenities. Even when your husband is your biggest cheerleader, it's just different.

The fear isn't only about cancer coming back. Once you've looked death in the face, you change. There's a part of you that never wants to go back to who you were before.

Things look different in every way. In nature, the skies are more beautiful, not just at sunrise or sunset, but even when covered in clouds. The rain smells like purification. And it's not just nature that looks different; it's people.

The wonderful people who cross our paths, from healthcare providers and friends to strangers. I know people say and do things I disagree with, but now I find myself wondering why. What have they experienced that made them that way? I don't always figure it out, but I try to approach life with love and understanding instead of judgment.

New lens on work, leadership, and purpose

I remember my first day back at work after medical leave. The doctor told me to start slow and work my way up to full-time, but I didn't listen to those instructions. I was too excited.

All I could think about was the cancer patients who never got the chance to come back. So, I attacked that first day like a bear emerging from hibernation, full speed ahead. I worked more than eight hours, just filled with energy and gratitude.

The next morning, I could barely get out of bed. That was my lesson. "Start slow and work your way up to full-time," isn't just good advice. It's survival.

In the weeks and months that followed, I learned to put my health first. Everything else - even work - had to wait its turn.

I started seeing leadership through a new lens. Before cancer, I thought strength meant pushing harder, speaking louder, and proving myself at every turn. After cancer, I realized real strength sometimes looks quiet. It looks like patience, perspective, and grace under pressure.

One day, I was in a high-pressure meeting where tensions were running high. People were talking over each other, trying to prove their point, and I could feel the old me rising up, ready to jump in and steer the conversation. But then something in me shifted. I sat still for a moment, watching the room, and realized that none of it was life or death. It was just another meeting.

When I finally spoke, my voice was calm and steady. I asked a few questions instead of giving the answers. The room quieted, and within minutes, everyone was listening and brainstorming again. The tone changed, and so did the outcome.

That was the day I learned something no corporate training could ever teach me: calm is contagious, and leadership doesn't always have to roar to be heard.

The Pivot

Although I wanted to tackle the world, my energy came and went. I had to refocus. Some days I could do it all, and others I could barely do a thing. Instead of beating myself up, I learned to listen to my body.

Our bodies are wise. They will lead us down the right path if we just slow down long enough to listen.

I've always had hobbies, no matter how many hours I worked. I started this book before the cancer diagnosis, but I paused it for over a year while I took care of myself. I also streamlined my career.

Instead of obsessing over every detail of every program, I learned to hire people I trust and support them fully. I still love solving impossible problems, but I don't feel the need to do it alone anymore.

Somewhere along the way, I stopped wasting time on old fears and thoughts of not being enough. Those thoughts still pop up sometimes, but I don't stay there long. I remind myself that I am enough, and I'm still here for a reason.

It took time to reclaim my joy. I never really lost my humor; that's what carried me through the fight and kept others comfortable around me. But joy took longer. I found it again when I came back to this book.

Writing became my therapy. I could work on it late at night or on weekends, and instead of draining me, it gave me energy. It reminded me that creation, whether in writing or leadership, has been my way back to joy. I wasn't writing to impress anyone but to reconnect with myself. I had started a story, and I needed to finish it.

I finally stopped wasting time chasing perfection. If you wait for perfection, you'll never get going. I don't mind stepping out first, even if I fall flat - like a pancake. At least I tried.

It's okay to make mistakes. No one is perfect, and the world isn't watching as closely as we think. Most people are too busy with their own lives, unless, of course, you faint in public. After that happens a few times, your embarrassment threshold rises significantly.

I've also stopped wasting time on things that don't matter. That doesn't mean I don't rest. Rest does matter. But I no longer give my energy to what drains me. These days, I pour it into what brings joy, peace, or purpose. And in that quiet focus, I started noticing something new taking shape, threads of my life beginning to reconnect.

Reconnecting the Dots

When you're forced to slow down, it feels strange, almost like a punishment. At first, it feels like failure. But if you stick with it long enough and realize that the alternative to slowing down might have been death, it starts to feel more like clarity.

In the quiet, I began to see the threads of my life connect: the little girl who loved to create and entertain, the young woman who helped others find their beauty, the leader who led with heart, and the fighter who refused to give up. It all started to make sense.

Maybe I wasn't supposed to rebuild the old version of myself. Perhaps I was meant to grow into something new - a new kind of leader who doesn't just manage projects but inspires others to lead bravely.

And once that realization came, it wasn't just about healing anymore. It was about calling.

The Chair Lift Challenge

Not long after I started reconnecting the dots in my life, I found myself at the top of a mountain, literally.

It was a typical week in the Knoxville office. We had a client in town for several days and had worked our meeting schedule like a Rubik's cube to carve out time for an afternoon adventure.

The client really wanted to see a bear, so the team brainstormed several options. Eventually, we landed on a nice little trip up a mountain for some relaxation, beautiful scenery, and a bit of shopping.

It sounded magical. I was all about it, except for one little problem. To reach the top, you had to ride a chair lift.

Now, that sounded peaceful and fun to most of the group, but to me, it triggered full-on panic. I don't like heights, and I don't like hanging from open spaces.

That evening, I called home to share the plan. My family immediately said, "Mom, you need to tell them you don't do well with heights."

I replied, "How can I write a book called *Bravely Leading* if I'm too scared to put my butt in a chair lift with the client and the team?"

So, I made up my mind, I was going to do it.

The next day, we headed off on our adventure. We had a blast on the way there, even stopping at a Buc-ee's to show the client what it looks like to buy a Christmas tree at the same place you fill up for gas. But when we arrived at our destination, I could feel my nerves start to tighten.

We paused at the bottom to take pictures. I smiled for the camera a little longer than usual, mainly stalling for time as my anxiety climbed right alongside the mountain. Before I knew it, my mouth was so dry I could hardly talk, and I was sweating like someone had dumped a bucket of water on me. I told everyone what I was feeling, but I still insisted on getting on.

One of the ladies volunteered to ride with me. She said she was the oldest and would help keep me calm. And she did beautifully. In a crisis, I'd want her by my side any day.

At first, I was doing okay. I didn't love the little shake each time we went over a pole, but I was breathing through it. Then, the lift stopped.

The wind picked up. The chair swayed. And the silence was deafening.

Suddenly, I wasn't brave anymore. My heart raced, my breath shortened, and my mind filled with every dramatic possibility known to man. I tried to speak, but what came out was a strange, guttural noise, somewhere between a scream and a deep breath.

My seatmate was an angel. She patted my hands and said softly, "You're ok, you're ok." Then, out of nowhere, she asked, "Do you have any hobbies?"

Hobbies? I couldn't think of a single one at that moment, except the one I was living. So, I started telling her about this book.

And that's when I learned something powerful: Fear doesn't always hit when you're moving fast. Sometimes it finds you in the stillness, when you finally stop long enough to feel everything you've been holding in.

Eventually, the lift started again, slow and steady, carrying us higher. When we reached the top, I jumped off that chair like my life depended on it. It took a while for my pulse to calm and my shaking to stop, but eventually, I laughed.

That's when it clicked: courage isn't pretending you're not afraid. It's breathing through the stillness until you can move again.

Later, I looked back at that mountain and thought, *okay, lesson learned. Maybe the next climb won't scare me as much, or perhaps it will.* Either way, I knew this: there will always be another mountain, another still moment, another chance to choose courage and to choose who's in that chair lift with you.

The Calling

I started this book as a love letter to my daughters. I wanted them to have something to guide them through their careers, to know they could build a life of courage, leadership, and joy.

But when cancer came and the book was paused, that purpose shifted.

I still want them to read it, but they lived most of it right alongside me. The message grew bigger.

Now, I want to help anyone who's ever wrestled with anxiety, fear, or self-doubt while trying to build a life they're proud of.

I often think about Southern girls like me, born in small towns with big dreams. Girls who are taught to be polite, proper, and humble, but who also carry sparks bright enough to light up the night sky. I want them to know the world needs their voices, their ideas, and their courage.

And it's not just for southern girls. It's for anyone who's ever felt small, overlooked, or unsure they belong in the room. I want them to see that they do belong and that bravery has many accents, faces, and stories.

My career has allowed me to touch thousands of lives, hopefully in positive ways, but this book lets me cast a wider net. I want to share real stories, with all their humor, heartbreak, and healing. I want to help others move forward, even when life feels too heavy to carry.

This has become my calling. It's what I was born to do.

It's not just about telling stories. It's about helping others become the best version of themselves, sooner rather than later.

I'm looking forward to speaking to as many audiences as I can reach. Public speaking still scares me more than anything, but that's how I know it's my next step. The point of fear is the point of magic.

The truth is, we all have a calling, something that stirs us, challenges us, and scares us just enough to grow. Mine happens to be writing and speaking, but yours might look entirely different. Part of my purpose now is helping others find theirs and to push them to be brave enough to move through the fear. Because it never entirely goes away, we just learn to walk with it.

Stop waiting for permission or validation from people who can't see your vision. You don't need anyone else's approval to become the best version of yourself. That dream was planted in you for a reason. Move toward it anyway.

The Ongoing Journey

I'm not sure where the rest of my journey will take me.
Some days, I look at my accomplishments and think, *now that's a fantastic life, something to be proud of.* Other days, I look through a different lens and think, *I've barely scratched the surface of what I'm meant to achieve.*

But here's what I know for sure: God didn't take my life. He left me here. On borrowed time, for a reason.

And I don't intend to waste it by being mediocre.

I want to be great. I want to do things that seem impossible.

Maybe there are new dreams I'm just beginning to dream, or maybe a fresh path will unfold tomorrow.

Whatever it is, I promise you this. Just as I once promised my daughters, I won't be too scared to step onto that path, even if it seems wild or out of reach to others.

The Challenge to Readers

You don't have to go through a health crisis to pivot your own life story. Every single day, you get a chance to choose bravery.

Don't sit on the sidelines watching your own life pass by. Get in there, play the game, and make your own calls. No one else knows the dreams and passions living inside you. It's up to you to name them, nurture them, and chase them down.

We're all scared of something. Fear shows up differently for each of us. Spend some time figuring out what yours looks like, then work on building up the unique talents that'll help you get through it.

Most importantly, don't let fear keep you from living, I mean, *really living*, your best life. Move forward with courage, face the challenges that will shape you, and remember that's how greatness begins.

I've learned that bravery doesn't always look like standing tall. Sometimes it looks like showing up scared, tired, or unsure, and doing it anyway.

Bravery isn't the absence of fear; it's choosing authenticity over comfort, one step at a time.

Wherever you are right now, know this: you already have everything inside you to rise, rebuild, and bravely lead.

Lessons Learned from Chapter Twelve

Fear will always be there. Move anyway.

Your worth isn't tied to titles, paychecks, or approval. It's tied to who you are and how you show up.

Authenticity attracts the right people, opportunities, and joy.

Lead with courage, but also with compassion for yourself and others.

Healing and growth take time. Give yourself grace as you rebuild.

Purpose isn't found in perfection. It's found in persistence.

Bravery isn't about never being scared. It's about showing up, scars and all.

Closing Passage

Life doesn't always go as planned, but Lord, it sure knows how to teach you. I've learned that courage isn't always loud, and strength doesn't always roar. Sometimes, it's the quiet voice whispering, "Get up, honey, you've still got more to do."

Each ending we face is a beginning waiting to be discovered.

My story is still unfolding, and so is yours.

Wherever life takes you next, may you never let fear stop you in your tracks or dull your shine. The world needs your light, your story, and your bravery.

Because in the end, leadership isn't about titles, timelines, or trophies.

It's about impact - the lives you touch, the laughter you share, and the light you leave behind.

If my story reminds you of anything, let it be this: you can be strong and soft, bold and kind, polished and perfectly human, all at the same time.

I don't know what's ahead, but I trust the same God who's got me this far. I've learned that grace shows up in the hardest places, that laughter really is medicine, and that bravery can look like getting up just one more time than you fall.

Wherever you are in your story, keep getting up.

Keep believing.

Keep shining.

Keep laughing.

And keep moving—even through the fear.

Love, Mom

Gratitude

To my daughters — you are my greatest teachers in courage, resilience, and joy. Watching you grow, stumble, learn, and rise through your own journeys has been one of the greatest gifts of my life. I wrote this book hoping you'd see your mom do the same—not perfectly, but always honestly. You come from strong women, and you carry that strength in every step you take. May you trust your voice, honor your gifts, and always chase the dreams that whisper to your heart. And above all, my sweet girls... I hope you dance.

To my parents — thank you for the foundation you gave me, the love that steadied me, and the belief you poured into me long before I understood my own strength. You taught me to work hard, play hard, laugh often, and take pride in doing things the right way. Your example became the quiet confidence I carried into every room.

To my husband — the silent support and constant love in my life. Thank you for being my steady place, my calm in the chaos, and the person who holds space for me, even when I can't express what I'm carrying. Your patience, encouragement, and quiet strength have grounded me through every high and low. You've given me the freedom to chase big dreams, rebuild when life required it, and keep moving forward when fear tried to hold me still.

To my brother — my first best friend and the person whose example still pushes me to be better. You have been a steady presence through every chapter of my life, showing me what strength, integrity, and resilience look like in action. You are a remarkable brother, son, father, grandfather, and entrepreneur, and I've admired you for as long as I can remember. Thank you for believing in me, challenging me, and loving me through every version of myself. Your life continues to inspire me more than you know.

To the strong women who shaped my life — Nana, Mamaw, Aunt Betty, and every woman who pulled up a chair and made room for me. You taught me to lead with kindness, humor, and grit. You showed me that women can build extraordinary lives without shrinking to fit anyone's expectations.

To the women I met along the way — the business owners, the mentors, the miracle-workers behind the scenes. Thank you for showing me what generosity in leadership looks like. You proved that success doesn't require sharp elbows; it requires open hands.

To every colleague, leader, and teammate who believed in me, challenged me, or trusted me with big, impossible programs — thank you. You taught me how to navigate chaos, manage pressure, and find joy in the work.

To the people who showed up during my hardest seasons — the ones who sat with me in fear, prayed with me in uncertainty, and celebrated with me in every small victory. Cancer changed my life, but you helped change how I lived it.

To my family and friends — the ones who helped me breathe when life felt heavy and laugh when I needed it most. Thank you for reminding me of who I was on the days I forgot.

And to the reader — thank you for giving my story a place to land. If even one page gives you permission to rise, rebuild, or take one brave step forward, then every moment of writing this was worth it.

Thank you, from the deepest part of me, for being part of this journey.